ASQ FOX VALLEY
Section 1208

The ASQ
Supply Chain
Management Primer

Also available from ASQ Quality Press:

A Practical Application of Supply Chain Management Principles
Thomas I. Schoenfeldt

The Supplier Management Handbook, Sixth Edition
ASQ Customer-Supplier Division; James L. Bossert, editor

Complex Service Delivery Processes: Strategy to Operations, Second Edition
Jean Harvey

The Executive Guide to Innovation: Turning Good Ideas into Great Results
Jane Keathley, Peter Merrill, Tracy Owens, Ian Meggarrey, and
Kevin Posey

The ASQ Auditing Handbook, Fourth Edition
J.P. Russell, editor

*Principles of Quality Costs: Financial Measures for Strategic Implementation
of Quality Management, Fourth Edition*
Douglas C. Wood, editor

Performance Metrics: The Levers for Process Management
Duke Okes

Root Cause Analysis: Simplified Tools and Techniques, Second Edition
Bjørn Andersen and Tom Fagerhaug

*The Certified Manager of Quality/Organizational Excellence Handbook,
Fourth Edition*
Russell T. Westcott, editor

The Quality Toolbox, Second Edition
Nancy R. Tague

*The ASQ Quality Improvement Pocket Guide: Basic History, Concepts, Tools,
and Relationships*
Grace L. Duffy, editor

*The Internal Auditing Pocket Guide: Preparing, Performing, Reporting and
Follow-up, Second Edition*
J.P. Russell

To request a complimentary catalog of ASQ Quality Press publications,
call 800-248-1946, or visit our Web site at http://www.asq.org/quality-press.

The ASQ
Supply Chain
Management Primer

J.P. Russell, Editor

ASQ Quality Press
Milwaukee, Wisconsin

American Society for Quality, Quality Press, Milwaukee, WI 53203
© 2014 by ASQ
All rights reserved. Published 2013.
Printed in the United States of America.

18   17   16   15   14   13   12   5   4   3   2   1

Library of Congress Cataloging-in-Publication Data

The ASQ supply chain management primer / editor, J.P. Russell.
    pages cm
Includes bibliographical references.
ISBN 978-0-87389-867-6 (hardcover: alk. paper)
1. Business logistics. I. Russell, J.P. (James P.), 1945-
HD38.5.A87 2013
658.7—dc23

                        2013037474

Acquisitions Editor: Matt T. Meinholz
Managing Editor: Paul Daniel O'Mara
Production Administrator: Randall Benson

ASQ Mission: The American Society for Quality advances individual, organizational, and community excellence worldwide through learning, quality improvement, and knowledge exchange.

Attention Bookstores, Wholesalers, Schools, and Corporations: ASQ Quality Press books, video, audio, and software are available at quantity discounts with bulk purchases for business, educational, or instructional use. For information, please contact ASQ Quality Press at 800-248-1946, or write to ASQ Quality Press, P.O. Box 3005, Milwaukee, WI 53201-3005.

To place orders or to request ASQ membership information, call 800-248-1946. Visit our Web site at www.asq.org/quality-press.

∞   Printed on acid-free paper

Quality Press
600 N. Plankinton Ave.
Milwaukee, WI 53203-2914
E-mail: authors@asq.org

The Global Voice of Quality™

Contents

List of Figures and Tables

Foreword

The *ASQ Supply Chain Management Primer* is an investment by the American Society for Quality's Customer–Supplier Division (CSD) into the quality body of knowledge (QBoK™) and member value. Indeed, the inspiration for this text came when we were searching on how we could best serve our members worldwide. I believed that placing this supply chain management fundamentals book in the hands of all our divisional members would permit a developing step in both our technology and community. I asked Dennis Arter, a key leader in the development and dissemination of customer–supplier theory and practice in ASQ's Customer–Supplier Division, and he agreed. Together we approached J.P. Russell, asking him to gather subject matter experts and provide the leadership required to bring the book together. In true community fashion, a call went out to the Division's immense resources. The call was answered and their gifts of wisdom were poured into writings. JP then performed the skilled work of a master project manager and created a common voice and flow from the individual contributions.

Appreciations go out to the contributing authors and CSD leadership. Both made this project possible. Also, thanks to Sue Daniels for her copyediting and to Quality Press resources, especially Matt Meinholz.

I trust you will find *The ASQ Supply Chain Management Primer* informative and applicable to your daily work. CSD remains dedicated to the mission of providing answers that develop, improve, and strengthen customer–supplier relationships. As a volunteer leader-based community, we welcome members to jump in, be involved, and share their knowledge of best practices. Our community strength is sourced from each of you.

Stephen K. Hacker
Chair of ASQ Global Advisory Committee and ASQ Chair-Elect 2013

Notes to the Reader

The Use

This primer provides a foundation for supply chain management. It may be used by executives to understand the risks and strategic issues surrounding global sourcing. It is also for purchasing professionals new to the idea of supply chain management as an enterprise within an organization. It can also be used as a review for supply quality specialists or as an introduction for personnel involved in the supply chain management process.

It was written with the assumption of operating in a free and competitive environment.

The Contents

The primer is organized by first presenting common processes used to purchase goods and services. Our aim is to cover basic fundamental responsibilities and duties for each process. Historically, many of these activities operated independent of one another. But as the number of suppliers has increased and their geographic locations have expanded globally, added inefficiencies and risks surfaced.

The last chapter of the book brings together the individual methods plus other tasks necessary to manage a global supply chain. Because of our approach there is some necessary redundancy, but the degree of detail varies according to the focus of the chapter. For example, we introduce the SCOR model in a couple of early chapters but it is not discussed in detail until Chapter 7.

Obsolescence management is included in the appendix because it goes beyond basic or fundamental supply chain management.

The Glossary

Originally we did not plan to include a glossary, but as the supply management field evolved so has the vocabulary and new words and phrases have been introduced to better describe certain actions or tasks. If no appropriate definition existed, the authors created one. The definitions were reviewed, edited, and added to the glossary to help in the understanding of supply chain management. The first instance of a glossary word is italicized within the main text.

Acknowledgements

Authors

Dennis Arter (primary author Chapter 1)

Zubair A. Khurshid (primary author Chapters 3 and 5)

Helen Kiesel (general topic author and contributor)

Jodi L. Medley-McMahon, (primary author Chapter 6)

Akio Miura (primary author Chapter 2)

Paul Myerson (primary author Chapter 7)

Dan Reid (primary author Chapter 4)

Once the ASQ Customer–Supplier Division leaders approved the project, a call went out for contributors. The above persons volunteered their time and expertise to join ASQ and the Customer–Supplier Division in an effort to provide a supply chain primer to fill a growing worldwide need. These experts and practitioners provided the fundamental knowledge needed to craft this book. We are thankful and appreciative of their contributions, patience, and responsiveness to queries. The primer is designed to be a starter document for developing fundamentally sound supply chain networks.

Reviewers

Beatriz Fuentes Castañeda, Qualified ISO/TS internal auditor and MMOG internal auditor

Mark Durivage, ASQ Fellow, CMQ/OE, CRE, CQE, CQA

Dick Gould, ASQ Fellow

Elias Monreal, ASQ-CQIA, CQPA, CMI, CQT, CSSGB, CCT, CQA, CQE, CMQ/OE

Teresa A. Whitacre, CQA, CQE, CQM/OE, CSSGB, ASQ Fellow

The final development steps of the project involved a peer review to make sure the information in the primer is credible and to identify technical issues. We thank the above reviewers for taking their valuable time to review and comment on the draft manuscript. The reviewers pointed out a need to reorganize the primer to better align with project objectives.

About the Authors

Dennis Arter is an author, consultant, and trainer from Kennewick, Washington State, United States. He earned a bachelor's degree in chemistry from the University of Illinois and became a nuclear submarine officer. After military service, Arter wrote *Quality Audits for Improved Performance,* a best seller published by ASQ Quality Press. He teaches and publishes on auditing, management systems, and risk. Arter is an ASQ fellow, certified quality auditor, and former member of the ASQ Board of Directors.

Zubair A. Khurshid, PE, is a management and quality consultant, adjunct faculty member, and guest speaker to executive programs. He holds a bachelor's degree in electrical engineering and a master's degree in engineering management. He is a senior member of ASQ and is certified by ASQ as a Six Sigma Black Belt and manager of quality/ organizational excellence. He is also a member of IEEE, APICS, and the Project Management Institute. Professionally he has contributed in various management positions to partner and vendor strategy, ISO 9001, Six Sigma, program management, corporate governance, and processes spanning capital and operating budgeting, tender and contracts, invoicing and payments, material management, and service provisioning in the Middle East and Pakistan.

Helen Kiesel is an ASQ senior member, certified quality auditor, RABQSA AS9100 AIEA auditor, and RABQSA quality management system lead auditor. She is a quality systems manager for Goodrich Corporation, with 24 years of aerospace quality experience. Kiesel has developed, implemented, and maintained quality management systems that are certified to ISO 9001 and AS9100 since 1995. She is responsible for supplier quality and audits and for facilitating suppliers' efforts in achieving ISO 9001 or AS9100 certifications. Kiesel was the first recipient of the *Quality Systems Update* magazine's Management Representative of the Year Award.

Jodi Medley-McMahon is the quality and productivity manager for the Management Association–MRA's Institute of Management and a certified principal auditor through RAB-QSA International. McMahon has 25 years of managerial and engineering experience with multi-national enterprises in several industries, including electronics, plastics coatings, flexible packaging, and software development. She is a consultant and instructor for MRA, a senior member of ASQ, and a member of the Project Management Institute. She holds undergraduate degrees in biology and chemistry and a master's degree in engineering management.

Akio Miura is an ASQ fellow, certified quality auditor, certified quality engineer, certified manager of quality/organizational excellence, certified reliability engineer, certified Six Sigma Black Belt, certified biomedical auditor, certified HACCP auditor, and certified software quality engineer He has been a quality management consultant since the 1980s and has helped more than 100 companies in Japan and some in the United States establish management systems and attain certification to the ISO 9000 series, cGMP, API Spec Q1, MIL-Q 9858A, QS-9000, and other major standards in the 1990s. Miura has been an RAB/IQA-approved lead auditor training course instructor since 1993 and an active contributor to ASQ discussion forums since 2004.

Paul Myerson has more than 30 years of experience in supply chain strategies, systems, and operations. Myerson holds a bachelor's degree in logistics from Pennsylvania State University and an MBA in physical distribution from Temple University. He has an extensive background as a supply chain professional, consultant, teacher (currently an adjunct professor at New Jersey City and Kean Universities), and author. Myerson is the author of *Lean Supply Chain and Logistics Management* (McGraw-Hill, 2012) and currently writes a column for *Inbound Logistics* magazine and a blog for *IndustryWeek* magazine on the topic of lean supply chains.

Dan Reid, an ASQ fellow and certified quality engineer, is best known as an author of QS-9000, ISO/TS 16949, ISO 9001, and ISO IWA-1. While at the Automotive Industry Action Group, he led successful projects for effective problem solving, cost of poor quality, and supplier management. Previously at General Motors Corporation, among other assignments he led or supervised more than 40 lean workshops, was the first leader of the International Automotive Task Force, and established a supplier quality function at the GM Service Parts Division.

1
Supply Chain Management Briefing

Supply chain management is a system. Like all systems, it is composed of many connected processes, all working in harmony to achieve organizational objectives. There are five basic activities we must implement for superior achievement of those objectives. The processes in typical sequential order are:

- Define your requirements.
- Select a *supplier*.
- Award the business.
- Build and strengthen relationships.
- Monitor the performance.

These five activities apply to all organizations, be they government, industry, healthcare, or education. They form the basis of this primer.

DEFINE YOUR REQUIREMENTS

Three things must be defined before you can obtain the goods and services you want:

1. *Technical requirements.* These involve classic form, fit, and function. For manufactured and process items, requirements are usually communicated by a combination of drawings, *specifications*, and standards. In the service sector, requirements are often specified in a statement of work.

2. *Accept–reject criteria.* Often, we need certain tolerances in machining or certain percentages in a blend. The work must be performed within a certain period of time. These criteria are measured and communicated through certificates, reports, and inspections.

3. *Management system requirements.* For those few suppliers *critical to product or service,* we need to specify the management system(s) to be used when performing the work. Management systems can come from government regulations (such as FDA manufacturing practices), international standards (such as ISO 9001 and spin-offs), national standards (such as ASME's boiler code), or industry standards (such as the Joint Commission's for hospitals and the American Petroleum Institute's for pipelines). Smaller suppliers can pick and choose from portions of bigger documents, as appropriate. These standard or custom system requirements become the foundation for suppliers' site-specific manuals, procedures, and assembly sheets.

Of course, all these requirements (technical, accept, and management) must be spelled out in a *contract* or *purchase order (PO)*. To keep contract instruments reasonably small, we often call out these common documents by reference or attachment. Many government and business organizations use standard supplier terms and conditions. They use addenda for customizing (adding or subtracting individual requirements). To conserve time, energy, and resources, we often place these common requirements on a server accessible by suppliers and potential suppliers. The common PDF format is normally used for these electronic files.

SELECT A SUPPLIER

Over time, providers of goods and services build up a reputation. This reputation may be for price, durability, variety, or any number of different attractors for that supplier's chosen market:

- Customers learn about this reputation through experience, in that they see their components in other assemblies they have worked on.

- They learn about this reputation through professional engineering societies, such as quality or mechanical or plastics.

- They learn about this reputation through their marketing, in print and in television and in electronic media.

- They learn about this reputation through recommendations from a trusted friend or professional colleague, or from customer feedback ratings.

- They learn about this reputation through a sales agent or a *distributor.*

All of this input allows customers to develop a list of possible suppliers. This may be called a bidders list.

Next customers need pre-award data for making their selection from the list of possible suppliers. A common way to obtain these data is to send out a request for bid to four to six possible suppliers. This is called the short list. The functional specifications (without proprietary information) are sent, along with quantity and delivery date estimates. If the suppliers wish to perform the work, they send a bid back to the customer. Many types and pieces of information are included, so the customer can make an informed decision:

- These data can take the form of catalog descriptions. Suppliers will often produce attractive print catalogs. They make these catalogs available to potential customers at trade shows. They give the catalogs to sales agents and distributors. Many suppliers now put catalog information online on their company websites. Often these catalogs can be downloaded as PDF files for sharing and study by the engineers. It is very unusual to see any proprietary information in catalogs, but general specifications, photos, dimensions, and capabilities are commonly shown.

- Pre-award data can come from people-to-people conversations. Suppliers often have sales staff members on duty around the clock to answer technical and pricing questions from existing and potential customers. Some suppliers hire outside sales agents, who are assigned to cover a geographical territory. They call on existing and potential customers to provide answers. Sales agents usually receive pay based on the number of calls they make and the sales they generate. This is called a commission.

- Pre-award data can come from answers to written surveys (called questionnaires) sent by the customer to the possible sources. Today, many of these questionnaires are sent by e-mail or placed on the customer website for potential suppliers to complete online. A survey that was useful 10 years ago may no longer be valuable today.

- Past performance history can be used to make a supplier selection. If the item worked without problems before, it is likely to work again in the same environment.

- Sometimes the customer's customer has provided a list of pre-approved sources to use. This promotes efficiency in that the decision work has already been done. It also promotes consistency in that these pre-approved suppliers are known performers. The practice of pre-approving sub-suppliers is common in the automotive and aerospace industries.

- For really important items or services (high cost, critical to production or performance, or having risk of failure), customers may need additional data. Some customers may ask their suppliers to be certified through conformity assessment registration programs. ISO 9001 is the most common certificate for quality. For high-value purchases, when quality and reliability are very important, the customer may send a small team of experts to the potential supplier's factory. This team will conduct an on-site, pre-award survey of the top two or three possible sources before making a final decision. Some industries (automotive especially) will use first-article inspection methods. A small quantity of items are purchased and then subjected to intense testing at the customer site. If those tests are favorable, then large quantities will be ordered. For services, an organization may try the service for a trial period or for a small project.

Once the data are analyzed, the acceptable supplier is placed on an approved supplier list. This allows the supplier to be used again for future work without the need for deep analysis.

AWARD THE BUSINESS

The buyer (sometimes called purchasing agent or contracting officer) makes a purchasing decision, often in consultation with engineering, quality, safety, environmental, and risk professionals. If a bid was not obtained earlier, it is requested now. In contract language, this is called the offer. The supplier is offering goods or services to the customer for a specific price and with specific terms. In the United States, this practice is part of the Uniform Commercial Code, commonly called contract law. It is similar to the *United Nations Convention on Contracts for the Sale of Goods,* which has been ratified by most nations of the world.

Once an offer is received, it is accepted by issuing a purchase order. The purchase order is signed by the buyer, on behalf of the officers of the customer. This then becomes an offer to the supplier, who signs the purchase order and sends a copy back to the customer. So, there now are an offer and acceptance from the supplier, and then an offer and acceptance from the customer. There is now a binding contract (see Figure 1.1, Simplified supplier process). Later modifications to the contract, such as increasing the quantity or changing a specification, come from the customer as a change order. This is an offer to the existing supplier, who accepts the new terms.

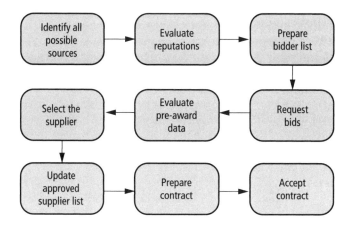

Figure 1.1 Simplified supplier selection process..

BUILD AND STRENGTHEN RELATIONSHIPS

Supplier relationships have always been important but not fully explored until modern times. Historically the relationship with a supplier may have been reduced to that of one with the supplier with the lowest price. This approach focused only on immediate, short-term benefits to the buying organization rather than on long-term, comprehensive benefits to the buying organization. In many cases the low-price mentality was in conflict with customer expectations and may, as a result, have created conflict and mistrust.

Today, purchasing organizations should use a more holistic strategy to ensure they are receiving the best overall value for their money. For some goods and services, viewing suppliers as partners in meeting customer needs may create ongoing opportunities for improvement.

Some of the following aspects may be a factor for building and strengthening supplier relationships:

- Capacity and locations: Fewer suppliers means lower administrative costs to monitor them.

- Lead times and on-time delivery history: Lower inventory lowers costs and shorter lead times mean greater flexibility.

- Defect history: Few complaints and investigations mean lower costs.

- Ability of the supplier to negotiate price and access raw materials.

- Environmental, societal, and organizational stewardship.

- Technical capabilities and knowledge transfer.

- Flexibility and ability to customize.

The individual supplier relationship strategy should be consistent with an overall organization supplier strategy. An effective strategy should include provisions for supplier development, alternate sourcing, information sharing, and collaborative design activities and should be based on a long-term sustainable relationship.

The prime objective of the supply chain is to maximize overall value to the customer organization. In some cases the only way to achieve the maximum value is to establish supplier relationships for a win-win strategy.

MONITOR THE PERFORMANCE

Most codes and standards, prudently, do not require audits of suppliers. Auditing is but one of the many methods used to monitor supplier performance. Going from the easiest and least expensive to the hardest and most expensive, the ways to monitor performance are:

- *Certificates and other paperwork.* Although they are often used interchangeably, there is a difference between a certificate of conformance and a certificate of compliance. The former states an inspection or test was performed and the result was in conformance with stated form-fit-function requirements. The latter states the work done to make the part or perform the service was in compliance with all required drawings, specifications, procedures, manuals, standards, and regulations. Of course, this cannot be determined with 100% accuracy, so a certificate of compliance has little value. On the other hand, copies of tests performed on the item prior to ship can be of high value to the customer. These material test report copies are easy to include with the shipment and cost the supplier little extra money.

- *Inspections.* These are performed by the supplier prior to product shipment. They include in-process and final inspections. The cost, size, or complexity of the job sometimes causes the customer to send an inspector to the job site before shipment. A large roadway bridge span would be easier and cheaper to correct at the factory rather than at the bridge construction site. These source inspections are performed by employees or agents of the customer. They can be quite costly. When the customer chooses to inspect the material after it is delivered, it is called receiving inspection. Smart organizations are applying statistical methods as well as automation to reduce the cost and effort of these inspections. For commodity items produced in other countries, the customer will sometimes require conformity assessment. Shipments are inspected and tested by qualified (accredited or certified) personnel working for an authorized third-party agent. Both parties (customer and supplier) agree to accept the test results.

- *Registration.* To reduce the burdens on both suppliers and customers, a worldwide program to register suppliers to international management system standards was developed in the 1980s. The idea was for all customers to accept a single supplier certificate. The already-established conformity assessment program was used. These third-party registrations certify management systems to be conforming to international standards and provide confidence to the customer that goods and services will conform to their requirements. They do not guarantee that products or services are conforming to customer requirements, however, nor do they verify that process methods are technically sound. The supplier pays for this registration service.

- *Technical site visits.* These are usually informal visits by scientists, engineers, or function managers to the supplier site. Their purpose is to improve communications and strengthen relationships. For goods, the visit focuses on process and product details. For services, the visit focuses on capabilities and service expectations. Site visits may not provide contractual direction, which must come from the authorized purchasing agents.

- *Audits.* Critical and important suppliers may benefit from a formal visit by customer auditors every one to three years. These on-site reviews (or remote virtual reviews) examine systems, processes, and products. Their purpose is to provide assurances that the supplier's necessary controls have been defined and implemented. Audits also determine whether those controls actually work and will remain after the audit had been completed. These audits are classified as second-party audits. (First-party audits are internal audits; third-party audits are done by regulators and registrars.)

Supplier scorecards and *dashboards* are common tools used to keep track of the overall state of individual suppliers. They are often presented during management review meetings.

THE ENTERPRISE PROCESSES

Organizations continue to focus on core competencies. This is resulting in more dependence on high-quality materials and services from suppliers. There is no time in history that supply chain management (SCM) has been more important to ensure that organizations (private industry, nonprofit, government, and education sectors) can survive in the global economy and network communities.

For some organizations, SCM is a complicated enterprise or collection of processes that must be managed. The knowledge and skills go beyond establishing materials specifications and asking the purchasing or procurement department to seek quotes or tender offers. There may be a global network, and meeting customer demand may depend on first-, second-, and, perhaps, third-tier suppliers. The SCM enterprise needs to be organized to avoid unnecessary risks and to ensure organization objectives are achieved.

A formal model called the Supply Chain Operations Reference (SCOR) model will be discussed in Chapter 7. It is a commonsense way of defining, understanding, measuring, and improving the various supply chain processes. It applies to all organizations, be they for-profit, nonprofit, governmental, or nongovernmental. The SCOR model is based on five general management processes: plan, source, make, deliver, and return.

The enterprise processes may be integrated into an existing management system or standalone function. The enterprise organization processes must answer the following questions:

- How must the logistics network be managed?
- How should product development and technology issues be addressed?
- How will supply match customer demand forecasting?
- How will risk factors be incorporated into decisions?
- What resources are needed to manage the enterprise?

2
Define Requirements

Many organizations implementing a supply chain management system are already sourcing parts, materials, equipment, and services. Defining needs and requirements actually starts in the original design of product, service, or process.

GENERAL CONCEPTS OF PROCUREMENT CONTROL

Scope and Objective of Procurement Control

Procurement or purchasing control should be applied for all materials, components, parts, and services to be purchased, procured, or out-sourced and then used, consumed or incorporated in the organization's final product or service. This is not only to ensure good final product or service quality, but also to ensure the quality of the organization's own procurement function.

Procurement control consists of the activities or processes for defining product or service requirements, evaluating or assessing suppliers, maintaining approved supplier lists, controlling order placement, accepting ordered items, and change management. It may be applied to equipment, parts, and materials to be used for the organization's own purposes as well as for manufacture of customer items or delivery of a service to a customer.

The purchasing of equipment to be used for a production or service operation process should be controlled through a predetermined method such as the equipment and materials control procedure. The purchasing of office supplies should be controlled separately.

Purchasing should be based on total value rather than just initial price. A supplier with the lowest quoted price may not present the lowest cost to the organization (supplier's customer) if defect costs and loss of customer goodwill are considered.

Defining Requirements

The processes to define requirements may include the following steps:

- The organization specifies requirements.

- The organization requests quotations from potential suppliers.

- The suppliers review the requirements and submit offers or solutions to the organization.

- Organization personnel review the offer and start negotiations.

- A supplier is selected.

- A contract, purchase order information, or other agreement is issued to the supplier.

- The supplier reviews the order requirements and, if satisfactory, accepts the terms and conditions.

- The supplier and organization monitor compliance to terms and conditions.

- The supplier reports any changes and their effects on the organization.

- The organization renegotiates as needed to meet objectives.

The customer organization should document the process for establishing a relationship with a supplier. The documentation should include required records. Establishing an agreement forms the basis for making changes for amendments or adjusting to market changes. Requirements for *traceability* and proper authorizations should be defined.

The organization must determine all the requirements related to the product or service being purchased. Some requirements may be critical to the form, fit, or function of a product. Requirements may be characteristic or performance based, or both. Requirements may relate to the organization's belief that process thinking leads to a product or service that meets specified requirements. Process requirements may be based on a direct measurement such as temperature and dimensions of an object. There also may be statutory and regulatory requirements or additional requirements not stated but known and considered necessary by the supplier. Table 2.1 shows examples of requirements.

Characteristic/ performance	Storage/ delivery/ distribution	Documen- tation	System/ process	Safety/ environment	Testing/ inspection
Dimensions	Conditions	Instructions	SPC targets	Hazardous vapors	First article
Weight	Turnover	Disposal	Management system standards	Water or air pollution	Source inspection
Height	Refrigerated truck	Identification	Training	Disposal	Sampling plan
Tolerances	Mode of delivery	Bar code	Design	Warnings	Test methods and equipment
Activity	Delivery time	Drawings	Qualifications of personnel	Protective equipment	Certificate of compliance
Strength	Maintenance in storage	Technical data	Audits	Emissions	
Biological characteristics	Shelf life	Records retention		Social responsibility	
Hardness	Size, placement and required information on the label	Origin			
Viscosity		Customs			
Solubility		QAR code			
RPMs		Returns			
Speed	Shipping requirements				
Size					
Fatigue					
Response time					

Table 2.1   Product service requirement examples.

Requirements and needs will vary from organization to organization based on the nature of the product or service. Requirements must be measureable and how they will be measured should be specified; for example, response time in minutes or weight in kilograms.

In contracts requiring supplier engineering or design activities, determination of the requirements should be initiated through fact finding, question and answer sessions, or information exchanges with stakeholders or other interested parties. Data gathering practices include interviews, questionnaires, user observation, use cases, and prototyping.

Thus the organization has to issue the procurement or outsourcing contract specification as complete as possible. If a supplier receives an order verbally but does not have the order requirements documented, it is possible that the supplier will get into trouble at a later date by not meeting expectations. The supplier should confirm the order requirements before acceptance by documenting the contract terms and specifications in some appropriate manner with a signature and submitting it for confirmation. The descriptions should be clearly referenced when ordering.

Purchasing information describes many aspects of the product and services to be delivered by the supplier. The information may describe various requirements but is not limited to the following:

- Description of the product
- Quantity
- Delivery due dates
- Agreed on price, rate, or fee
- Approval of product, procedures, processes, and equipment
- Qualification of personnel
- Management systems such as those for quality, safety, environmental, and *risk management*
- Relevant drawings and process data (technical data), and revision level
- Requirements for test specimens
- Record retention
- Sub-tier supplier *flow-down requirements*
- Notification of changes of management or management systems
- Right of access
- Notification of nonconformances
- Shipping, labeling, and packaging requirements
- Product shelf life and age control requirements
- *First-article inspection*
- Source inspection
- Certificate of conformance, analysis, or compliance requirements
- Payment terms such as invoicing, timing, and method
- Shipping requirements including imports, exports, and customs
- International traffic in arms regulations and Export Administration Regulations requirements
- Identification and traceability requirements for possible recall and investigation

These requirements are identified in different manners. The requirements can be distributed to the supplier on a separate supplier requirements document, which is then referenced in the purchase order, contract, or agreement. In some cases the requirements are stated directly on the purchasing document, which suppliers should review to ensure they can satisfy the stated requirements.

The supplier is not obligated by contract to satisfy expectations of the organization if they are not properly identified and is not bound by contract to any requirements that are not documented. If there are any ambiguous, deficient, or inaccurate supplier flow-down requirements, the supplier has to contact the organization (supplier's customer) to gain further detail for clarification prior to accepting the order, because such ambiguous requirements can put both the organization and the supplier at risk.

When an order is placed with a supplier for any product or service, the organization should give the supplier the clearly written specification with sufficiently detailed description of needs and requirements as well as terms and conditions (the output of the design control program).

It is very important to ensure that the supplier has received, reviewed, and acknowledged or confirmed the requirements. By doing so, the organization will have a greater degree of confidence that the supplier is capable of fulfilling the order requirements. If the purchasing requirements are not properly managed, this will have a cascading negative effect on delivery, cycle time, quality, and cost throughout the supply chain.

DESIGN

Every product and service was designed or created at some point in time. For new products or processes, documentation about product and service requirements and needs should be available. For existing products and service, design documents may have been lost or not maintained. Nevertheless, requirements and needs start with design.

Design Output Information

Design outputs specify the characteristics of the designed product, service, or process that are essential for safe and proper functioning (for example, operating, storage, handling, maintenance, and disposal requirements) and contain or make reference to acceptance criteria in documents or model prototypes.

Design outputs should provide appropriate information for purchasing, production, and services. These should be formally captured, recorded, reviewed, and approved prior to release.

Design Validation

According to the definition in the current good manufacturing practices (cGMP) of the Food and Drug Administration, *validation* means "confirmation by examination and provision of objective evidence that the particular requirements for a specific intended use can be consistently fulfilled. Product design validation means establishing by objective evidence that device (product) specifications conform to user needs and intended use(s)."[1]

Design validation is carried out at the final stage of design review, following successful design verification.

As processes become more automated, it is increasingly necessary for the organization to know that the supplier's software and robots will work as intended. Human controls (operators and inspectors) are being replaced by machine controls. Parts and material flaws may be unknown until a product recall is necessary. This is especially important for outsourced processes in a highly regulated industry in which the organization is ultimately responsible for obeying laws and regulations.

Newly designed products, services, or processes should be validated before they are released for the actual production or application.

Design Changes

All design changes should include evaluation of the effect of the changes on constituent parts, kits, and linked processes. The review of design changes should also include the effect of changes on existing services and product already delivered.

If any change or modification is made to an existing process, the process has to be revalidated after the change.

CONTRACT/ORDER REVIEW

The objective of contract review by the organization is to ensure that the contract requirements are adequately defined and the supplier has the ability to meet the defined requirements.

This review ensures three things:

- Order requirements, including delivery schedule and the requirements for delivery and post-delivery activities such as handling, storage, installation, operation, and maintenance, are adequately defined and documented.

- Contract or order requirements differing from those previously expressed are resolved.

- The supplier has the ability to meet the defined requirements.

Many low-risk and common products or services are purchased based on supplier catalog descriptions. Even for such products or services, however, the descriptions should be clearly referenced when ordering.

If a supplier received the order verbally but does not have the order requirements documented, there will be the possibility the supplier performance will be unsatisfactory and result in a dispute or legal action.

The supplier should confirm the order requirements before acceptance by documenting the contract terms and specifications in some appropriate manner with the supplier's signature and submitting it for confirmation.

> **Contract Review Example**
>
> In an international tender in Singapore for a plant construction project, the company the author worked for was not the lowest bidder but was awarded the contract. As the manager for all technical matters for that project, the author used his own procedures and checklists for contract and design review. With such procedures and checklists, he found many mistakes in the customer tender specification and notified them of this fact. This satisfied the customer and as a result, his company was deemed the best in meeting the customer's technical requirements. There was no price negotiation. From such experience, the author recognized that contract review is really useful and important, in fact, indispensable both for customer and supplier.

After clarifying every contract requirement, the organization's responsible manager should prepare the specific quality plan for each contract, incorporating all special or unusual requirements into the company's basic quality plan for the product or service and providing for the flow-down of all pertinent provisions of the contract to all applicable functional areas, including first-tier and *sub-tier suppliers.*

Amendments

When the organization changes product or service requirements, suppliers need to know about the change. These changes are normally amended to the original contract as a change order.

> For customized products such as chairs, every order must be reviewed and verified due to lot-to-lot or batch-to-batch variations in color, size, mechanisms, fabric, and ergonomics.

Reference

1. Process Validation, Food and Drug Administration, www.fda.gov/MedicalDevices/ DeviceRegulationandGuidance/PostmarketRequirements/QualitySystemsRegulations/ MedicalDeviceQualitySystemsManual/ucm122439.htm (case sensitive).

3

Select Suppliers

SUPPLY CHAIN BACKGROUND

A supply chain includes suppliers, manufacturers, distributors, system integrators, service providers, value-adding retailers, and consumers.

Suppliers are a group providing raw material, machines, services, spare parts, and other inputs. There can be different suppliers for different parts or for the same part or service. Manufacturers are those who shape and name the product in the supply chain. Distributors are those who provide networks from one place or more for distribution to retailers. Distributors may also provide warehouse or storage services. In particular, companies dealing in fast-moving consumer goods depend on distributors to reach retailers. Service providers offer services in the form of consultancy, tasks, training, feasibility, development, projects delivery, and more. Value-adding resellers enhance the product or service branding, image, wrapping, *bundling*, and packaging with additional features and sell them directly to the customers or through retailers. This is a generic supply chain.

In addition, the supply chain can include logistics suppliers, financial institutions, human resource specialists, contractors, enablers, and others.

SUPPLY CHAIN COUNCIL AND THE SCOR MODEL

The Supply Chain Council (SCC) was established in 1996 with 69 founding member organizations. It is a global nonprofit organization (supply-chain.org), and the membership number has reached about 1,000. SCC's membership consists primarily of practitioners representing a broad cross section of industries, including manufacturers, services, distributors, and retailers. SCC has developed and endorsed the Supply Chain Operations Reference-model (SCOR) as the cross-industry standard for supply chain management.

The supply chain of every organization includes a combination of five basic SCOR processes: plan, source, make, deliver, and return. The only difference is what type of strategy the company is following. For example, is it following sourced from stocked or sourced from ordered? A combination of all these processes will provide a building block for the supply chain, and their combination from suppliers to the ultimate customers represents the whole supply chain.

For manufacturers, there are three sources:

1. Make to stock.
2. Make to order.
3. Engineer to order options.

For customers, there are another three:

1. Source to stock items.
2. Source ordered product.
3. Source engineered products.

For delivery, there are yet another three:

1. Deliver of stock items.
2. Deliver of make to order.
3. Deliver engineered to order.

ORGANIZATIONAL REQUIREMENTS PLANNING

Organizations have processes for planning their material and item requirements. These are known as material requirement planning (MRP) and manufacturing resource planning (MRP II). The materials management department carefully analyzes a forecast and rationalizes it according to the on-hand material availability in warehouses. Historical trends are observed before finalizing the requirements. Cross-functional teams are engaged to finalize the requirements, which are then sent to the procurement, purchasing, or contracting department for purchasing. For purchasing of strategic items that have high risk and criticality, requirements are prepared in a comprehensive document known as a *request for proposal (RFP)* or similar title.

Depending on the strategy, an organization decides whether to produce the product, provide the service, or outsource it. This strategic decision is supplemented by information such as total cost of ownership, taking into account the organization's area of core expertise and business or operations model.

SOURCING

APICS, The Association for Operations Management, defines sourcing as the process of identifying a company that provides needed goods or services.[1] This process entails identifying, qualifying, and negotiating agreements with suppliers of goods and services. It also includes the acquiring of technology, labor, intellectual property, and capital.

Sourcing is the first of the five processes in the SCOR model. Sourcing is a vital activity in the supply chain to ensure an organization can make optimum supplier choices in its own best interests. Sourcing is deployed in all organizations regardless of whether they have a downstream flow of products or services.

Purchasing organizations use this process to find, evaluate, and select suppliers for both direct and indirect materials. Direct materials are related to the product manufacturing process or process for providing a service. Indirect items describe other products and services that are needed to run the company. In accounting terms, many organizations classify costs as direct and indirect. Direct costs are the costs for items such as parts or chemicals used to create the end product or service provided by the organization. Indirect costs are the costs indirectly related to the end product or service provided by the organization, such as office or cleaning supplies.

Types of Sourcing

There are three types of sourcing: sole, multiple, and single. If the organization has a choice of only one source for supply, this is sole sourcing. This could be due to various factors such as raw materials, technical specifications, location, the fact that only one organization produces the item, or the fact that another department of the same organization is producing the item. This type of sourcing is the best candidate for partnering. For example, a medical device organization may need a specialized resin to make a plastic part for a device.

Using two, three, or more suppliers for the same item or items is multiple sourcing. Orders are normally shared with them in proportion to their performance in terms of price, quality, delivery, and other organizational requirements such as environmental performance or social responsibility. This leads to competition, which subsequently brings better quality, lower costs, better service, and improved *sustainability*. This type of sourcing also helps in eliminating disruption of supply due to strikes, shortages, and other problems. However, multiple suppliers for the same service or part may cause variation in the final product or service as well as traceability issues.

If an organization opts to use only one supplier from several available, this is a single sourcing strategic decision for which partnerships and long-term contracts are needed. With guaranteed large-volume business, the supplier dedicates its resources to improving the process. For the customer, single sourcing brings reduced organization and production costs, single accountability, supplier loyalty, and better product with less variation. However, risks become high for delivery disruptions. Due to economies of scale, the supplier has advantages in being single supplier, enjoying new orders from the same customer and reduced costs of operational processes.

> **Single source example**
>
> A company decided to single source its steel requirements to save costs and reduce variation in gage and type of steel, but it once had to reject several coils of steel, and the supplier could not react on time to replace the material and avoid disruption of the production process.

Single sourcing results in a drastic reduction of a supplier base while creating the opportunity to improve supplier quality. One major company reported that it eliminated 90% of its suppliers and improved supplier quality from 92% to 99.97% through single sourcing.

Sourcing Strategy

Whether to have sole, single, or multiple sourcing is a strategic decision since no one sourcing strategy approach can meet all requirements. This fact leads to a situation in which the purchasing strategy for a particular item or service will affect the strategy followed during the supplier evaluation and selection process.

Initially, many assumptions are made while developing the sourcing strategy. Nevertheless, because of market dynamics, users' preferences, and organizational objectives, there may be many subsequent changes. The assumptions developed during the strategy phase should be reevaluated during the actual selection process. Thus the selected sourcing strategy also affects the selection and evaluation process. The organization should consider the following elements and associated risks during the development of the sourcing strategy:

- Single versus multiple supply source.
- Shorter versus longer contract time commitment.
- Suppliers with design proposals versus suppliers without design proposals.
- Full-service versus non-full-service suppliers.
- Domestic versus international suppliers.

- Complementary or barometric relationship expectations. Complementary relations are long-term ones based on mutual trust and helping each other make improvements. Barometric relations are situational or short-term ones in which the nature of the relationship changes with the changes in market conditions and other factors.

Spend Analysis

It is necessary to study and evaluate current purchase spending over the years in order to find opportunities to reduce costs and enhance value. *Spend analysis* provides information about the following:

- Total spending
- Spending by category
- Suppliers' identification of each part, material, tool, service, or other component
- Spending per supplier per category
- How to leverage spend to reduce direct and indirect material costs
- Possibility of reduction of usage
- Risk in the spend

Total spending thus can be broken down into categories and subcategories. These could include raw materials, insurance, fleet, freight, facilities, or operations. Raw materials, for instance, can perhaps be subcategorized to chemicals or moldings. Facilities could be subcategorized to office supplies, furniture, services, staffing, warehousing, utilities, HVAC, or fixtures. High-value spending categories and subcategories are identified with tools such as Pareto analysis. Suppliers for categories and subcategories are identified, improvement opportunities are assessed, and category strategies are formulated for maximum leverage, cost savings, and risks mitigation.

Spend analysis is also substantiated by the premise that a unit of reduction in spending is equivalent to a 3X to 5X increase in margins and profits. This means efforts to reduce spending on purchased items or services have a significant effect on overall costs.

If all functions of an organization use one supplier, for example, that would increase the bargaining power of the organization when negotiating for a lower price. Other spend analysis methods include demand reduction, substituting cheaper products, and segmenting suppliers to manage important commodities effectively.

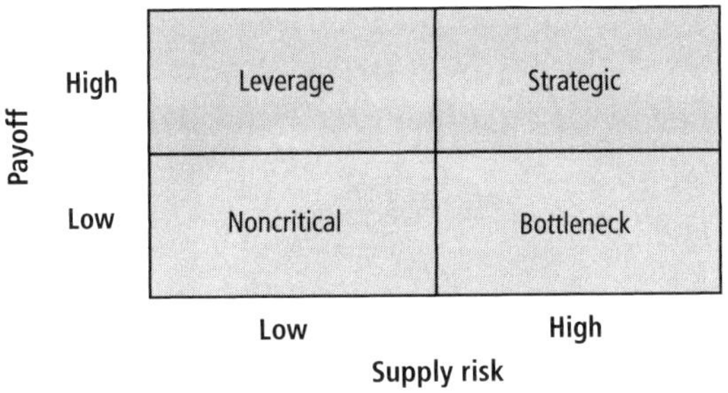

Figure 3.1   Purchasing portfolio matrix.

A purchasing portfolio matrix was developed by Peter Kraljic in 1983. This can be used to segment suppliers for items, prioritize and mitigate risks, and leverage buying power. Products or services can be grouped in four quadrants in purview of profit impact and supply risks (Figure 3.1).

A different sourcing strategy can be formulated for each category:

- *Noncritical* items have low value and several alternative suppliers, therefore risk associated with noncritical items is low. Noncritical items need efficient processing, product standardization, and inventory optimization. Office supplies and janitorial services can be an example of such items.

- *Leverage* items are high in price and thus enable buyers to exercise their purchasing power. Raw material for primary products and labor supervisory services are examples of such items.

- *Bottleneck* items have low value but have supply chain risk in terms of sourcing. Bottleneck items have high risks and low profit, and these risks can be lessened through risk mitigation strategies. Some products from the construction industry and on-site construction are examples of such items.

- *Strategic* items have high value and provide competitive advantage for the organization. These items are provided by few suppliers. Strategic items need a lot of focus and attention and may require strategic partnerships. Examples include service installations, design of drawings for construction, technology infrastructure, and consultancy services.

Tactical Sourcing

Day-to-day ordering activities are carried out by procurement, purchasing, or contract departments. These are pre-order and post-order activities such as issuing purchase orders or receiving deliveries. To supplement these activities, tactical sourcing activities (see Table 3.1) can be done in conjunction with purchasing activities. Following are some of the tactical sourcing activities:

1. Market research
2. Commodity analysis
3. More accurate demand forecast requirements
4. Price and cost analysis

Market Research

It is important to watch market dynamics. Ongoing mergers and acquisitions could altogether change the supply chain scene, making consolidated suppliers more powerful and ultimately affecting terms. Similarly, a shortage of items resulting from natural catastrophes or abrupt market breakdowns could raise prices.

Commodity Analysis

Either product or service *commodity* items may make up the lion's share of an organization's sourcing budget. The organization therefore might employ an expert in the respective commodity purchase to carry out commodity analysis for sourcing in that category.

Serial no.	Activity	Performed actions	Areas to be considered
1	Market research	Market analysis and predictions and suppliers' organizational level movements for future positioning	Mergers and acquisitions, shortages and government policies
2	Commodity analysis	Analysis of commodity to be purchased in terms of value and volume	Sourcing decisions for the particular commodity
3	More accurate forecasting requirements	Accurate forecast by cross-functional team with less error combined with seasonal, trend, cyclic, and time considerations	Inventory optimization with better lead time and reduced inventory costs
4	Price and cost analysis	Analysis of the value being purchased in terms of supplier cost, quality, and service	Best purchase output

Table 3.1 Activities in tactical sourcing.

More Accurate Demand Forecast Requirements

Having more accurate forecasts results in higher supplier efficiency that leads to reduced cost and improved service for both the supplier and purchaser. Usually a cross-functional team of subject matter experts works with the sourcing team members to determine demand and supply with downstream customers that are ultimately provided to upstream suppliers.

Price and Cost Analysis

This is of prime importance. Supplier cost, quality, and service should be continuously analyzed to benchmark the supplier against its competitors using the same criteria. This establishes that the organization is achieving best output from its purchase.

STRATEGIC SOURCING

APICS defines strategic sourcing as a comprehensive approach for locating and sourcing key material suppliers.[2] It often includes the process of analyzing total spend for material spend categories. There is a focus on the development of long-term relationships with trading partners who can help the purchaser meet profitability and customer satisfaction goals. From an IT perspective, strategic sourcing includes automation of *request for quotation (RFQ)*, *request for proposal (RFP)*, electronic auction, and contract management processes.

Once a make-or-buy decision (services may be provided internally or externally) has been made and requirements have been defined, the next step is to find suppliers and start the sourcing process. The requirement document could be an RFQ or RFP. The terms generally mean the same thing. In the Internet era, finding suppliers is easier and quicker than it was earlier, but be aware there are counterfeit components, items, and parts to be avoided. Here are some ways of finding appropriate suppliers:

- *Supplier websites:* Almost every supplier maintains a website featuring its profile, products, and services. These websites, products, and services are registered with search engines, and a quick list of suppliers can be accessed by typing appropriate words into the search.

- *Supplier information database:* Supply, purchasing, or procurement managers usually maintain a database of various suppliers with respect to their profiles and areas of expertise. This includes current, past, and potential suppliers for work at hand. This information is a ready reference for identification.

- *Supplier catalogs:* Supplier catalogs usually contain plenty of information about the suppliers, the products and services offered and, sometimes, prices. Managers can use them for studying the supplier portfolios and estimating total costs.

- *Trade registers:* Trade registers contain information about suppliers and their financial standings. These are a good source of information and can be found in hard copies and online or CDs. These registers are indexed by commodity, manufacturer, trade name, and trademarks.

- *Trade journals:* Trade journals report the latest trends in an industry and contain supplier advertisements. Digital and Internet editions are now also available.

- *Phone directories:* Earlier, phone directories were in hard copies. Now they are electronic, searchable, and available online for quickly finding supplier contact information.

- *Sales personnel:* Supplier sales personnel visit many companies and have much information about suitable solutions to different requirements. They can readily suggest appropriate products or services. Their sales presentations frequently contain valuable information.

- *Expos and trade shows:* Regional and international expos and trade shows are excellent opportunities for supply, purchasing, or procurement managers to learn about new products and services and their sources. These events usually are sponsored by suppliers, customers, and other parties in the supply chain.

- *Company functional experts:* Another source of information is the purchasing organization's own staff. Functional department staff members frequently have knowledge based on their professional training, memberships, and attendance at workshops. Regular meetings with these people are opportunities to learn about new suppliers and channels.

- *Professional organizations:* Networking with personnel from other organizations, particularly through professional associations, is an excellent source of information about suppliers.

- *Current suppliers:* Current suppliers engaged with the organization should be explored first when sourcing new items. This also could lead to supplier development.

SOURCING ALTERNATIVES

There are sourcing alternatives choices that may be explored after identifying potential suppliers. Some sourcing choices include:

- Manufacturer or distributor
- Local, national, or international supplier
- Large or small supplier
- Single or multiple sourcing

Manufacturer vs. Distributor

Size of purchase, manufacturers' policies for direct sales, storage space policies, and the extent of services are determinants for selecting a manufacturer or distributor. An organization might, for example, purchase a product directly from a manufacturer due to product size or *volume*, or might purchase the same product from a distributor that can warehouse several products it uses and provide services it would otherwise need to purchase elsewhere. Other factors are the *original equipment manufacturer (OEM)* price and saving of distribution margins, and *vendor-managed inventory (VMI)* options for saving inventory costs. VMI is feasible for long-term contracts and is a consideration for creating an integrated supply chain leading to an outsourcing partnership.

Local, National, or International Supplier

Logistics and inventory costs, support, and responsiveness are the criteria for decisions on whether to choose a local, national, or international supplier. The just-in-time (JIT)[3] concept works with local suppliers, although international suppliers set up and incorporate local offices as required by some customer organizations. Another consideration will be the ongoing costs of developing and maintaining the relationship. These include travel costs to visit the supplier and perform inspections, audits, or problem-solving investigations.

Large or Small Supplier

Analysis of diversity plans, bargaining power of suppliers and customers, and forward integration are the determinants for this choice.

Single vs. Multiple Sourcing

Reducing the supply base and selecting one supplier generally leads to choosing a large supplier to assure continuous supply, yet having more than one supplier also has merit. Whether to have single or multiple suppliers is therefore a strategic decision.

OUTSOURCING

APICS defines outsourcing as the process of having suppliers provide goods and services that were previously provided internally.[4] Outsourcing involves substitution or replacement of internal capability and production by the organization.

Drivers for outsourcing are mainly globalization, increasing complexity, and emerging markets. The main reasons for outsourcing include more operating flexibility, reduced fixed assets, and high efficiency. Outsourcing may be a strategic or tactical decision. Once an organization determines that it does not possess the core competency to produce goods or a service, it may choose to outsource that item. An organization may choose to outsource a product or service to reduce costs and improve efficiency, or it may decide not to not outsource due to the strategic importance in terms of critically or risk of the product or service. Additionally, there are cost considerations between make and buy decisions. Organizational processes are also being outsourced. Many organizations are now thriving on their core competencies and preferring to use emerging business models to enhance profitability and maximize shareholder value.

There are associated risks with outsourcing that include loss of control, loss of client focus, lack of clarity, lack of cost control, ineffective management, and loss of confidentiality. These have to be carefully identified and assessed appropriately with tools such as failure mode effects analysis (FMEA) and mitigated through commensurate controls.

Critical Issues in Selecting Suppliers

Critical issues to be looked at prior to evaluation of suppliers include the following:

- *Size relationship:* The size of an organization compared to that of its supplier affects attention paid and bargaining power. Some organizations compare the annual dollar purchase to the supplier's total sales revenue and use that number as a selection criterion.

- *Offshore suppliers:* Selecting offshore suppliers requires careful inventory analysis of factors including replenishment and lead times. Another factor is the additional steps required during evaluation.

- *Countertrade requirements:* Countertrade is the exchange of goods or services that are paid for, in whole or part, with other goods or services rather than with money. Having a countertrade agreement in a sales contract may require the purchaser to source goods in another country, therefore substantially affecting the supplier selection decision.

- *Competitors as suppliers:* Future supplier development and relationship enhancement can be hindered when competitors are selected as suppliers due to lack of trust and absence of any sharing of confidential information.

- *Sustainability and diversity objectives:* Corporate social responsibility and legislative obligations can lead to purchasing from green suppliers and minority or female-owned enterprises.

- *Risk and reward issues:* Risks associated with lower-price suppliers and the ability of a supplier to ramp up production in case of large volume requirement are trade-offs. The decision requires development of a risk management program during the selection process.

Reducing a Supplier Base

The following three analyses can be used for reducing the supplier base so limited resources can be engaged for the evaluation of the shortlisted suppliers:

1. *Financial risk analysis:* Perfunctory financial analysis of a supplier is important. There are third-party providers who can report any problematic financial issues that could disrupt supply.

2. *Supplier performance:* Current suppliers' performance is an important input. Even though it could be related to providing another product or service, the information offers insight into performance.

3. *Suppliers' direct information:* Survey questionnaires and information requests can help the purchaser know the cost structures, technologies, quality performance, and other factors that can serve as qualifiers for shortlisting suppliers.

SOURCING DOCUMENTS

The customer can use a number of documents to initiate the supplier selection process. They may include:

- *Request for information (RFI).* Used to collect information from potential suppliers regarding products, services, and options.

- *Request for proposal (RFP).* Formal request for suppliers to submit a quote to supply a particular product or service.

The documents above may include information regarding:

- Product or service characteristics
- Product or service performance requirements

- Process validation and control expectations
- Identification of key characteristics
- Management system requirements
- Special requirements such as those related to environmental, security, or safety matters
- Record requirements such as build drawings or certificates

The design and engineering functions should also be included in a needs analysis. Supply chain needs are often driven by specifications produced by either of these functions in an organization. A minor change in a specification could significantly increase or decrease sourcing options.

The supplier chosen must be able to meet process specification requirements, such as a C_{pK} *minimum* (variation) on the supplied components or materials. A supplier may also be subject to the regulatory requirements that could be spelled out in the specification. If a supplier needs to achieve and maintain an accreditation, certification, or regulatory marks such as UL or CSA International, the customer has to know the supplier is capable of doing so.

Another consideration is whether the supplier has a documented and effective disaster recovery plan. It is important to the success of the customer that its suppliers be prepared to continue the supply chain even in the event of a fire, cyberattack, or natural disaster.

SUPPLIER SELECTION AND EVALUATION

After preliminary shortlisting, comprehensive evaluation is performed for selection of a supplier. Common and major steps followed are:

- *Evaluation of supplier's response:* This has typically been the sole traditional method of supplier evaluation and selection.
  A supplier's proposal or quotation is evaluated completely. It is useful for a cross-functional team to conduct these evaluations for technical and commercial compliance. Suppliers are ranked according to the predefined criteria, and this becomes a major contributor in deciding who is awarded a contract.

- *Supplier visits:* Supplier visits are a well-established way of checking and evaluating potential suppliers. Cross-functional teams from organizations visit the supplier sites with their checklists and determine the suppliers' strengths and weaknesses. Some visits may be done remotely using collaborative software technology via the Internet. Operation readiness assessments are a means to verify the supplier understands the requirements and is able to meet all customer expectations.

- *Preferred supplier list:* Preferred supplier lists (also called approved supplier lists) developed after meticulous analysis of supplier performance further simplify the evaluation and selection process. Many purchasing organizations maintain such lists of best suppliers for different products or services.

SUPPLIER EVALUATION CRITERIA

Primary factors for supplier evaluation are cost, quality, and delivery. The following supplier capabilities are also evaluated for critical items:

- Financial stability
- Management and employee capabilities
- Process and technological capabilities
- Cost structure
- Supplier quality, security, safety, and environmental compliance
- Production and scheduling system
- Supplier sourcing strategy
- Long-term relationship potential

Financial stability: Financial reports including liquidity, activity, profitability, and debt ratios should be checked and interpreted to ascertain the financial stability of supplier.

Management and employee capabilities: Abilities of key management personnel and employees determine the competitiveness of a supplier organization. Management interviews and histories of workforce turnover, strikes, and labor union activities may provide insight about the supplier capabilities.

Process and technological capabilities: Evaluation of suppliers' process capabilities involving design, technology, methods, and equipment, along with the capital equipment, competencies, and technology requirements are important and may include current and future processes.

Cost structure: If possible, it can be valuable to understand the supplier's costs. A common technique is to use reverse pricing to estimate those costs. Approximate values for direct, indirect, overhead, production, and process operating costs are examined to determine supplier efficiency.

Supplier quality, security, safety, and environmental compliance: Formal registration or self-declaration of conformity to industry, national, and international standards can be an indication of a supplier's management maturity. Commonly used standards include:

- Industry standards, such as the American Petroleum Institute, the Joint Commission (healthcare), the American Association of Blood Banks, and the Direct Marketing Association provide controls for a specific sector.

- Government standards, such as those of the U.S. Bureau of Engraving and Printing, U.S. Department of Defense, and the Centers for Medicare and Medicaid Services, are used by firms providing goods and services to those agencies.

- National standards, such as those of the American National Standards Institute (ANSI), Institute of Electrical and Electronic Engineers (IEEE), Canadian Standards Association (CSA), and British Standards Institute (BSI), cover a variety of business and government operations and are often precursors to international agreements.

- International standards, such as ISO 9001 (quality management), ISO 13485 (medical devices), ISO 14001 (environment), ISO/TS 16949 (automotive), AS9100 (aerospace), ISO 17025 (laboratories), OHSAS 18001 (safety), ISO 22000 (food safety), ISO 22301 (business continuity), ISO 27001 (information security) and ISO 28000 (shipping security), are used around the world.

- Guidance standards not meant for conformity assessment may also serve as an indication of a supplier's intent to act responsibly. Examples include ISO 26000 on social responsibility and ISO 31000 on risk management.

Production and scheduling systems: Beyond production technologies are the supplier's administrative and day-to-day operation controls. A purchaser may need to know if the production, inventory and delivery scheduling, and delivery systems are adequate to meet customer needs. It may be beneficial for the supplier and customer systems to be integrated for optimum sourcing.

Supplier sourcing strategy: The purchasing organization should also be aware of the supplier organization sourcing strategy risks. A single source strategy of a *critical part* or material by a supplier may represent an unacceptable risk to the purchaser. In some cases second- and third-tier suppliers may need to be evaluated.

Long-term relationship potential: The purchasing organization may have determined it is in their best interest to either develop a long-term relationship or not. The ability of the supplier organization to match an organization's long-term strategy could be an important factor in the selection process.

SUPPLIER EVALUATION AND SELECTION SURVEY

Supplier evaluation may also include rigorous and structured surveys. A survey should provide sufficient information to support a decision to keep or drop the supplier from further evaluation. Several areas may be covered in the survey, such as financial arrangements, organizational leadership, organization history, goods and services provided, current capacity, and important control systems. If used, these surveys should be less than 10 pages and should be easy to complete online. It is common to use generic survey forms for several potential suppliers.

APPROVED SUPPLIER LIST

It is common practice to create a list of qualified or approved suppliers. All qualified or approved suppliers should be in the approved supplier list (ASL). Suppliers may be restricted to only those on the list. Note that the term approved vendor list (AVL) sometimes is used instead of ASL.

Potential suppliers are approved or disapproved based on the quantitative assessment in the evaluation process. Approved suppliers may be periodically re-evaluated as part of performance management. This is discussed in Chapter 6.

Due to the passage of time and changes in markets and technologies, it may be necessary to re-evaluate approved suppliers. Re-evaluation of approved suppliers may include the following:

- Updating the initial evaluation criteria listed earlier

- Actual performance history such as on-time delivery; quality performance as received and in the field; history of past nonconformances; timeliness in submitting data, records, and responses to questions; ability to react quickly and effectively to solve problems; and performance and behavior in service

- Inspection and inventory control issues

- Shipping and transportation issues

- Changes in scope of goods and services, management, processes, and sourcing of materials

SUPPLIER CERTIFICATION

Customer organizations may qualify certain suppliers to a higher level called certified suppliers. This status is granted to the suppliers who consistently meet predetermined quality, cost, delivery, financial, and quantity objectives. Items from certified suppliers are not inspected, and these become *dock-to-stock* items. This substantially reduces inspection costs, providing assurance that high-quality levels remain intact. Supplier certification reduces the number of suppliers to a manageable level, thus further saving overhead costs.

Supplier certification is essentially a supplier development program. It might include a supplier's adherence to a particular standard or specify responsibilities of an organization's process design inspection procedures, statistical process control applications, and training, reporting, and correction procedures. Generally, it is oriented around the following three steps:

1. Qualifications
2. Education
3. Certification process

After certifying the supplier, the buyer organization also performs some tasks such as:

- Reviewing suppliers' critical manufacturing processes through control charts
- Setting up a minimal sampling inspection program
- Reviewing suppliers' quality reports
- Periodically visiting supplier sites

References

1. APICS, www.apics.org.
2. Ibid.
3. "Quality Glossary," *Quality Progress*, June 2007.
4. APICS, www.apics.org.

4

Award Contracts

Sourcing, contracts, and other purchasing decisions are at the tactical level of supply chain management, as are production decisions, inventory decisions, and transportation strategy.[1] When a customer has many potential suppliers and significant leverage, however, sourcing can also be a very strategic decision. A contract is a legally enforceable promise or set of promises made by one party to another. It is a legally binding agreement concerning a bargain that is essentially commercial in its nature and involves the sale or hire of commodities such as goods, services, or land.

PURCHASING FUNCTION

The purchasing (also called procurement) function in an organization has two primary and essential tasks: to select and contract with suppliers and to establish terms of purchased goods and services needed by the organization. Some organizations also assign responsibility for supplier development and improvement to the purchasing function.

Many organizations labor under the false belief that they have no options other than to buy from the first or, in some cases, their traditional supplier, and to pay the supplier's price. Some industries still have the luxury of passing costs on to one or more end customers or users. These are limited to industries in which customers have poor leverage, a concept that is discussed later in this chapter. Other industries do not have this luxury and have to work diligently on cost reduction and efficiency to compete.

Where the organization has an option, it is best to purchase needed products directly from the supplier that has the most "value add" in the product. For example, when buying a metal casting that must be subsequently machined, if the machining costs more than the casting, the organization should purchase from the machining company to maximize leverage. In some cases, it can make sense to purchase from distributors, but organizations will not have as much leverage on price with them as they will with original suppliers. There may be other benefits or reasons for using distributors, however. In the case of an electrical connector, the manufacturer will produce large quantities of connectors to achieve economy of scale. It may not be interested in selling small quantities of connectors to end users, so use of a distributor would be the best, if not the only option.

LEGAL ASPECTS OF PURCHASING

Since contracts are enforceable in a court of law, they are subject to regulatory requirements. These requirements can vary by jurisdiction. For purchases on which you can't afford to lose, you should seek legal advice from a competent source when developing terms and conditions to govern the transaction, including any remedies that may be needed.

The United States Uniform Commercial Code (UCC) is a set of statutes governing the conduct of business, sales, warranties, negotiable instruments, loans secured by personal property, and other commercial matters. It has been adopted with minor variations by all states except Louisiana.[2] The UCC is a model code, so it does not have legal effect in a jurisdiction unless UCC provisions are enacted by individual legislatures as statutes.

The UCC consists of rules of different transactional areas under articles based on types of transactions:

- Sales (amended Article 2)
- Leases (amended Article 2A)
- Negotiable instruments, previously known as commercial paper (revised Article 3)
- Bank deposits and collections (amended Article 4)
- Fund transfers (Article 4A)
- Letters of credit (revised Article 5)
- Bulk sales, previously known as bulk transfers (revised Article 6)
- Documents of title (revised Article 7)
- Investment securities (revised Article 8)
- Secured transactions (revised Article 9)

For supply chain management, these four areas are especially relevant:

1. Warranties
2. Transportation terms and risk of loss
3. Seller's rights
4. Buyer's rights

The United States UCC establishes each party's rights and obligations per common business practices based on the principles of fairness and reasonableness. Fairness and reasonableness also serves when a particular term is not defined in the contract. The law is not applicable outside the United States, but most other countries have similar commercial codes. English contract law is a body of law regulating contracts in England and Wales. It shares a heritage with countries across the British Commonwealth such as Australia, Canada, and India.

European Union (EU) law (commonly referred to as Union Law and historically called European Community law) is a body of treaties and legislation such as regulations and directives that have direct or indirect effect on the laws of EU member states.

The United Nations Commission on International Trade Law developed its Contracts for International Sale of Goods (CISG) treaty in 1980.[3] As of December 2011, it had been ratified by 78 countries. It is similar to the UCC.

COMPETITION

Competition in economics is a term that encompasses the notion of individuals and firms striving for a greater share of a market to sell or buy goods and services. A supplier that monopolizes the market for its product or service has no incentive to reduce cost or improve quality or service. Competition makes all competitors better because they have to improve to survive. Organizations should develop a number of potential suppliers for all critical purchased products. The efforts will pay off in both the short term and the long term. Even when an organization elects to award all its volume for a given purchase to a single supplier, having a number of bidders will ensure that the successful supplier understands the requirements and is providing a competitive price.

A practice is anticompetitive if it is deemed to unfairly inhibit free and effective competition in the marketplace. Examples include cartels, restrictive trade agreements, predatory pricing, and abuse of a dominant position.

TERMS AND CONDITIONS

Most organizations have a standard set of terms and conditions that will govern supplier relationships. These vary depending on the size of the organization, the annual spend amount, the amount of leverage the organization has, and regulatory requirements.

Potential suppliers need to take care in reviewing the purchaser's terms and conditions prior to signing agreements. Some purchasers include an evergreen clause, which means the contract will automatically be renewed unless one party disagrees, sometimes within a limited specified timeframe.

When there is potential for significant warranty or recall costs, agreement on any limitation of supplier liability for the remedies in the event of a purchased product or service failure should be agreed upon up front. Different industries handle warranty differently. In the passenger car market, the automakers provide warranty for their product, including purchased product for end users. In the heavy truck and aerospace industries, parts suppliers offer warranty to their customers' customers. This limits warranty liability to the *primes* or original equipment manufacturers (OEM) but shows up in higher piece prices for purchased products. Regulatory requirements may also specify how product or service guarantees or remedies will be handled for a specified industry or commodity.

When it comes to purchased product, it has been said that he who has the gold wins. Organizations with a large annual purchasing spend can dictate more terms and conditions than others. This is generally an advantage for the organization, but large organizations can fall into a trap of creating too many customer-specific requirements, which actually drive cost up. When a supplier has multiple customers in the same or a similar industry, meeting customer-specific requirements will require additional resources. The costs for these extra resources will have to be recovered from one or more customers.

Some purchasers now have environmental requirements for suppliers. The World Trade Organization (WTO) has cautioned that these can impede trade and even be used as an excuse for protectionism.[4] It adds that WTO member governments consider the protection of the environment and health to be legitimate policy objectives, and thus recommend taking an approach to help exporters meet standards and requirements.

To avoid proliferation of customer-specific requirements, organizations should participate and make use of any standards that are applicable and available. There are standards at the international, national, industry, and product levels. Standards development organizations such as the International Organization for Standardization (ISO), the American National Standards Institute (ANSI), the American Society of Mechanical Engineers (ASME), and SAE International offer many voluntary standards that organizations can use in specifications for their purchased products. Industry trade associations (for example, the Automotive Industry Action Group or AIAG) also produce harmonized customer requirements that can be used to avoid nonvalue-added costs in the supply chain.

UNDERSTANDING COST

Cost control is important to organizations. Cost plus margin equals price. Two main elements of cost control are cost estimating and actual cost tracking. Organizations have to account for costs and have a way of recovering them in their revenue. Some industries use competitive benchmarking and *tear-down* of competing products to better understand the design and estimate costs. This can involve tracking and use of data on costs such as raw materials and labor by region. At a minimum, organizations should estimate potential costs, then compare actual costs to the estimates and make adjustments to pricing or costs as necessary to ensure organizational commercial viability going forward.

Most sectors once operated with a pricing model based on cost plus margin. In sectors in which competition is significant, the pricing model has to be market based (for example, what customer organizations are willing to pay regardless of cost). This puts incentive on the producer to reduce costs to maintain or increase margin.

SPECIFICATIONS AND DESIGN RESPONSIBILITY AND APPROACH

Prior to the industrial age, customer organizations and suppliers were close enough geographically to do business personally, face-to-face. The industrial revolution created a proliferation of manufacturing organizations and purchased product requirements, which created a need for a new intermediary tool, the specification, to replace the direct communication between the customer and supplier. In its essence, a specification describes and prescribes requirements for a purchased product or service that can be used in a contract with a supplier.

In many sectors today, design responsibility for a product or service is with the supplier rather than with the customer organization. The party in the contract with responsibility and authority for establishing and maintaining the design records (for example, the specification) is responsible for the design. Where this is the customer organization, it is best to not over-engineer the design or specification up front. Even when suppliers are not responsible for the design, they often have valuable input to offer for design consideration. For example, they often can provide input that would improve the design or the cost of manufacture such as:

- The manufacturability of the design
- Establishing nominal and tolerances on dimensions, percentage of active ingredients, features, and various performance-related specifications
- Alternate materials or manufacturing processes

A supplier might have certain equipment and capabilities that influence the optimum design approach or requirements. When this is the case, the customer should send out a request for proposal (RFP) rather than a request for quote (RFQ) to solicit ideas from potential suppliers to incorporate into the final design for later quote. On the other hand, the customer should avoid specifications that only one supplier can meet. Competition will help control pricing and supplier performance over the life of the contract.

TYPES OF AGREEMENTS

There are several tools an organization can use to make an authorized purchase. These typically depend on the spending level and include:

- *Spot buys* (onetime purchases for special or emergency situations)
- Contracts (formal documented arrangements with a supplier due to risk)
- Expense reports (minor office and travel expenses charged against a budget)
- Acquisition cards (a preauthorized spending tool)
- *Evergreen contracts* (formal arrangements with a supplier that automatically renew)
- Blanket contracts with releases (formal arrangements with a supplier that require specific follow-up information before execution of the contract, such as releasing quantities over time)

TEAM SUPPLIER SELECTION

Purchased product often represents a significant cost to an organization. When this is true, the sourcing selection should be the result of work of a cross-functional team. The criteria for sourcing should include quality and service, as well as price. This requires the purchasing function to consult with and comprehend feedback from other disciplines such as quality, manufacturing, operations, risk, engineering, and after-market service in the sourcing decision.

NEGOTIATIONS

Chester Karrass is credited with saying, "In business as in life, you don't get what you deserve, you get what you negotiate."[5] Negotiation is a learned skill. While some are naturally better at it than others, all can benefit from some training in the art of negotiation. The results of your negotiations with suppliers will depend on your negotiation skills and your leverage. Because leverage is usually on the customer's side prior to an organization award, this will likely be the best opportunity to reduce cost of purchased products.

Buyer leverage is the amount of bargaining power buyers have when purchasing goods and services. The amount of buyer leverage relative to the bargaining power and leverage of the seller depends on the information seller and buyer have about the product, the relative scarcity or abundance of the product, the availability of product substitutes, and many other factors. In some cases there may be grants, discounts or government subsidies to promote trade for certain products or services or industry sectors. The relative leverage of buyers and sellers determines the price and terms of transactions and the nature of business relationships.

Many organizations work to create or improve leverage for their purchases. There are some things you can do to get a better deal for your organization. These include:

- *Part or unit number rationalization.* Part or item number proliferation fragments your total volume requirements across part or unit numbers and drives up cost by causing extra manufacturing setups, start-ups, changeovers, inventory, warehousing, scheduling, tracking, and servicing. When it comes to part or item numbers, fewer is better.

- *Bundling awards.* Organizations that make repetitive purchases or use several purchased products that could come from one type of supplier can create leverage by requesting bids on more than one item at a time or by sourcing one item number on a long-term contract rather than as a spot buy.

PURCHASE ORDER PROCESS

To secure good quality of purchased materials, adequate and complete documentation should be issued to the supplier. A signed purchase order is a contract. To start the purchase order process, an individual or group (operations, S4, engineering, district office) that requires the materials or components should prepare purchase requisitions and forward them to the procurement or purchasing manager. The purchase requisitions should reference the following:

- Material specifications with revision level
- Identification requirements
- Documentation requirements
- Need to send an inspector to witness source inspection

The purchase requisitions and purchase orders or contract must incorporate these important points:

- All technical documentation defining the products, such as standards, specifications and drawings, should be clearly identified, on the correct revision level, and enclosed when required.

- Adequate quality records, such as testing or inspection certificates, statistical process data, quality system certificate, and warrants, should be explicitly required in the purchase order.

- Requirements for notification of changes to source and/or composition of materials; manufacturing location; production, processing, or testing; certifications; or licensure.

- When purchasing toxic, hazardous, or otherwise restricted substances, the procurement or purchasing manager should include in the purchase order a request that the supplier provide a warrant or certificate that the substance and its packaging comply with governmental and safety regulations.

The procurement or purchasing manager should review and approve all purchasing documents prior to release, issue the inquiry to the suppliers on the ASL in accordance with the purchase requisition, and select and issue the purchase order to the most appropriate supplier. Routine or repeat purchases can be approved for a specified quantity or period of time (blanket purchase orders). Sufficient data on requirements for product characteristics or service specification should be clearly defined or attached.

CONTRACT RISK MANAGEMENT

Risk management and organization *continuity* planning should significantly drive purchasing contract strategy. When it comes to purchased goods and services, an organization can do a few things to mitigate risk. The following strategies have advantages and disadvantages:

- *Multiple sourcing.* Dual or multiple sourcing reduces supply risks, but it is expensive. When purchased product and services have to be qualified or validated, this requires redundant activities that drive up cost. It also divides the organization's total volume requirements over more than one supplier, which can result in forfeiture of any volume discounts. In a special case when the customer controls the design of a product, a dual set of tools, molds, or production equipment should be kept in a separate location to protect against potential disasters such as earthquake, fire, or flood. Having *tooling* and molds manufactured in an emerging market may be more cost-effective but may not provide comparable quality.

- *Build inventory.* Inventory is not a bad thing. Excess inventory is a bad thing, whether it is raw material, work-in-process, or finished goods. Excess inventory is one of the types of waste recognized by lean manufacturing, but carrying more inventory provides *safety stock* in case of an unforeseen problem. When customers elect to resource a current production part or material, building inventory to use while qualifying the new supplier is usually a necessity. Like multiple sourcing and dual tooling, building inventory can be costly. An organization should determine which of the options is most effective in mitigating risk at the optimal cost.

- *Qualify alternate part numbers or material.* This approach is used in industries such as commercial electronics in which several commodities can be readily and effectively substituted for a given application. This can also add cost by requiring multiple validations or qualifications. Many customers require suppliers to receive customer approval prior to shipping a new part or material to their locations. This requires the supplier to complete the customer-specific requirements for this approval, which also adds time and cost. In exchange, both the customer and supplier have a ready alternative if needed.

- *Supplier management requirements.* Contracts can include requirements to implement and maintain a management system certification. Assessment/certification of a supplier's management system gives the customer more confidence that the supplier will meet ongoing customer requirements but does not necessarily mitigate the risk of a sporadic outage or shortage.

Some sectors have developed sector-specific quality standards, such as ISO/TS 16949 (automotive), AS9100 (aerospace), and ISO 13485 (medical devices), with third-party certification requirements for suppliers. Use of standards as a baseline for supplier management can minimize cost to organizations but usually falls short of including all the customer-specific requirements they would like.

Contracts can also include requirements for the supplier to maintain a documented and effective disaster recovery plan or to demonstrate it is prepared for a fire, cyberattack, or natural disaster.

PERFORMANCE RULES

Supplier performance results (see Chapter 6) should be used by the customer to prioritize supplier development, establish an escalation or exit strategy, and influence future sourcing. Some customers effectively use contract incentives such as higher pricing for delivery by a specified date to drive better performance or, conversely, pricing penalties for missing a required timing deadline.

Supplier performance, including pricing, delivery, and service, is key to customer satisfaction. Customers and suppliers both need to work on it whenever possible. Open and timely communication and collaborative planning and problem solving are necessary to achieve the best performance over the life of a contract.

References

1. Environmental requirements and market access: preventing 'green protectionism,' www.wto.org/english/tratop_e/envir_e/envir_req_e.htm.

2. Legal Dictionary, http://dictionary.law.com/?wvsessionid=24d3d61befad4afabe1b0007d9c58ff0.

3. United Nations Convention on Contracts for the International Sale of Goods, http://untreaty.un.org/cod/avl/ha/ccisg/ccisg.html.

4. Environmental requirements and market access preventing 'green protectionism,' see reference 1.

5. http://leadershipquote.org/, April 2013.

5

Build Relationships

Supply chain relationship management activities can be subdivided into three macro processes: supplier relation management (SRM), internal supply chain management (ISCM), and customer relations management (CRM). When strategy is formulated, all three must be taken into account. Most organizations focus on only the ISCM process, which will not provide optimum results. To achieve superior performance, customer relationship management and supply chain management should be aligned.

SUPPLY CHAIN RELATIONSHIPS

In a supply chain, the purchasing organization cannot treat all the participants equally due to competitive positioning and scarcity of resources. Relationships with different participants should therefore be based on certain realities such as the percentage or the volume of orders, the nature of the product or service, and the availability of qualified suppliers in the present market.

If the product is a transactional one and can be readily purchased off the shelf in the open market, there may be fierce pricing competition among the suppliers to the extent that building strong relationships is probably not worth the effort.

Strategic goods and services, however, cannot be procured through arm's-length relations. Although cost must be a consideration, the focus must be on building collaborative relationships with a win-win approach.

SUPPLIER RELATIONSHIP MANAGEMENT

For the success of a supply chain, it is crucial to formulate an effective SRM strategy because it is related to the sourcing process. Unless high-quality material or service is sourced at competitive rates, it is unlikely that a product's cost and quality have a competitive edge in the market. SRM strategy must be in alignment with the overall supply chain strategy and support the competitive strategy. This becomes more important in light of the present market situation where the competition for market share through higher levels of customer satisfaction is becoming increasingly intense. Segments for different customer needs are being created, which increases product variety and the need for more customization. Exposures to quality global brands, increased flexibility and customization, and economies of scale achieved through reduced cost have made both responsiveness and efficiencies of supply chains even more important for success.

Globalization is reducing barriers to the movement of raw-materials, finished goods, technology, capital and, to some extent, labor. This increases investors' expectations of the supply chains in which they invest. A supply chain is like any other value chain, with its strength dependent on the strength of its weakest link. No supply chain strategy can work without a well-aligned SRM strategy that has sub-strategies for all the sub-processes of the macro process. An effective SRM strategy will have provisions for supplier development, alternate sourcing, information sharing, and collaborative design activities, and should be based on long-term sustainable relationships with suppliers.

The idea of SRM is not new, but the paradigms of conventional procurement procedures are very strong and have been difficult to change. These conventional procedures include lowest bidder to qualify, getting at least three bids for every item or service to be purchased, and emphasis on getting the maximum financial leverage from every deal, even at the expense of the other party. This approach focused only on immediate short-term benefits to the buying organization rather than on long-term, comprehensive benefits to the buying organization. For example, the purchasing or procurement function may find or negotiate a product or service price below what was budgeted, but the organization's subsequent processing costs increase or the organization's customer satisfaction or goodwill risks being undermined.

Slowly and gradually the concepts of long-term relations, win-win situations, total supply chain surplus, and mutual collaboration have crept in, enhancing the necessity of working on developing long-term, mutually beneficial collaborations. The prime objective of a supply chain is to maximize overall value to the customer organization. Value is the difference between the cost incurred in a supply chain and the worth the end product or service has to the customer. Supply chain surplus is when the value of the supply chain is correlated with its profitability.

CUSTOMER RELATIONSHIP MANAGEMENT

Customer relationship management (CRM) is another area that is very important for the success of a supply chain strategy because every supply chain strategy starts with customer requirement analysis and ends with customer satisfaction. The only thing constant about customer demand is that it is never constant. A successful CRM strategy can be built only through an atmosphere that supports innovation, customization, and personal relationships with customers while providing service, support, and new technology.

Historically, there has been a dividing line between the customer side (sales, marketing, and ventures) and supply side activities (purchasing, QC, and technical operations) in an organization. Modern times demand that organizations eliminate this dividing line and bring the groups together to advance the supply chain and improve their competitive advantage.

RELATIONSHIPS BASED ON CRITICALITY

When an organization in a supply chain is developing long-term sustainable relations with its suppliers, it requires resources. Due to limitations of resources, the same level of activities cannot be carried out for every supplier. Optimal results require prioritization based on:

- How much of the organization inputs are through a particular supplier.

- How critical the item or service being supplied by the organization is. If an item supplied by a supplier is critical to the organization, long-term mutual beneficial relations with this supplier are important to maintain uninterrupted supply.

- Whether the item or service is important in the finished product or service shipment (functional criticality).

- Criticality of an item in achieving the strategic objectives of the organization (strategic criticality).

COMPETITION AND STRATEGIES

Competitive pressures never remain the same in the market. These pressures do change, and the reasons they change have been explained in Michael Porter's five forces of competition model.[1] The five forces are: bargaining power of suppliers, bargaining power of customers, threat of new entrants, threats of substitution, and competition within the industry. These factors are normally different for different industries and are also product or service dependent. For instance, a high-margin product will attract more competitors than one with low margin. An industry requiring high initial investment and a heavy exit cost will attract fewer competitors than one in which entry and exit are relatively easy.

In the marketplace, there are always forces that oppose new entrants and forces that encourage them, but the fact is that competition conditions change with time and also with the product type and the stage of its life cycle. Availability and use of new technologies such as the Internet are also changing marketing dynamics. The competitive pressures normally result in more variety of products at competitive prices. This makes organizations think about changes in their competitive strategies, and the supply chain strategies have to be readjusted to cope with the new situation. Good supplier relationships can inhibit new entrants to the market and be a competitive advantage.

MANAGE SURPLUS INVENTORY AND MAXIMIZE AGILITY

The inter-company scope of strategic fit is essential today because the competitive playing field has shifted from company versus company to supply chain versus supply chain. Supply chain competition is like a relay race in which not only the speed of each runner is important but also the smooth transfer of the baton. This is analogous to the transfer of material, cash, and information in a supply chain. A company's partners in the supply chain may well determine the company's success as the company is intimately tied to its supply chain.

Taking this view requires that each company evaluate its actions in the context of the entire supply chain. This means treating a supply chain that a buying organization does not own as if it does own it. This assumption has led to a rash of changes in ownership of inventory from stage to stage in the supply chain. Buyer organizations have realized that if they force their suppliers to own the inventory, their costs will go down because they will not have to finance this inventory. In many cases, however, the suppliers simply take ownership of the parts inventory without making any changes in the way this inventory is managed. Because holding this inventory increases suppliers' costs, they are forced to raise their prices to the buyers or lower their margins. In the end, there is no real reduction in total cost because the supply chain merely shifts costs back and forth between its links.

Instead of just forcing the inventory on the supplier, the manufacturer and suppliers need to work together to actually reduce the amount of inventory that is required. By sharing demand information with the supplier, for example, the manufacturer can lower the amount of inventory needed in the chain, thus reducing overall cost in the supply chain and making the organizations in the supply chain better able to compete. The result will allow the entire supply chain to either increase profits by sharing the extra surplus or to reduce price by passing along some of the surplus to the customer.

In reality, the situation is much more dynamic as product life cycles get shorter and companies try to satisfy the changing needs of individual customers. In such situations, an organization may have to partner with many different suppliers depending on the product or service being produced and the customer being served. Organizations thus must think in terms of supply chains consisting of many players at each stage. The strategies and operations at organizations must be agile enough to maintain strategic fit in a changing environment. Furthermore, as customer needs vary over time, organizations must have ability to become part of new supply chains while ensuring strategic fits. This level of agility becomes more important as the competitive environment becomes more dynamic.

CUSTOMER-SUPPLIER VALUE CREATION PARADIGM

Using a value creation approach captures not only total cost considerations, but also performance advantages allowing the purchasing organization to create value for its customers and receive additional revenues that it otherwise could not. Within a customer–supplier relationship, the exchanged offerings are essential, as are the buyer's trade price, cost, and value information (especially concerning downstream effects). The basis for this interdependence is the resources that both companies possess. Value creation does not take place in isolation. The traditional value chain presumes that organizations buy a product, add value to this product, and then sell the product to the successor in the chain while asking for a return for the augmented value. Instead of adding value one after the other, the partners in the production of an offering create value together through varied types of relationships. This value is cooperatively created during the entire term of relationship with a supplier, but is most obvious in the research phase of product design when suppliers can help to create value not only for the customer organization, but also for the customers' customers.

The value of an offering can be augmented in three different ways:

1. An offering could directly reduce the related operating costs for the customer organization, which results in a value increase for this organization.
2. Operating costs for the customer's customer go down.
3. Revenue is enhanced due to the offering's superior value for the customer.

VALUE PROPOSITIONS

Value propositions are conceptual and pragmatic descriptions of what each partner expects to receive from others in the exchange process. Purchasers have a strategic vision of what they would like to accomplish long-term with a given partner. Purchasers should seek input from other departments or units within an organization regarding their needs and objectives. All supply partners must articulate the strategic picture they envision from the relationship. A precursor to this strategic vision is to carefully analyze the myriad choices from which to select the most appropriate value propositions. This analysis entails understanding, creating, and delivering value.

Value creation involves three fundamental tasks:

1. Developing new customer solutions or reinvigorating existing solutions
2. Enhancing the acquisition of inputs and their transformation into desired customer outputs
3. Creating and leveraging linkages and relationships to external marketplace entities, including channels and end users

Purchasers are simultaneously buyers and marketers with responsibility for developing long-term relationships that help solve problems throughout the relationship life cycle. Purchasers can develop new solutions for suppliers just as marketers have solved purchasing problems. This *quid pro quo* perspective is an integral part of relationship longevity. If these postures are maintained, value will be both created and sustained over time.

SUPPLY CHAIN MATURITY MODEL

A supply chain maturity (SCM) model is an approach to measuring and defining the relative maturity of defined supply chain elements of linkage, integration, and extension. Each of these elements is measured at the operational process level as a strategic, team-based, or operational process.

One SCM model includes three major pillars:

1. Managing relationships
2. Managing supply chain material flows
3. Managing information

In most cases, any lack of communication stems from a single root cause: a lack of alignment among organizational requirements, supplier and customer contacts, and information systems. Before embarking on an expensive supply chain system implementation, technology executives need to clearly delineate how the system will help close these gaps.

A clear case for improving supply chain performance begins by assigning costs to the consequences of poor communication. The diagnosis must be justified using quantitative metrics as well as qualitative symptoms and must include a treatment plan. Without translating supply chain solutions for reducing inventory and improving cycle times into financial terms, such as economic *value added,* managers stand little chance of convincing senior management to invest.

Many organizations today are deploying myriad procurement strategies, including:

- Applying *reverse auctions* to all commodities
- Applying strategic alliances for all commodities
- Outsourcing noncore processes that represent opportunities
- Leveraging and supply base reduction

SUPPLIER PARTNERSHIPS

Organizations are now reappraising their value chains and outsourcing activities they consider to be non-core. Simultaneous with this growth in outsourcing has been a move toward rationalization of the supplier base as organizations actively seek to reduce the number of suppliers with which they do business. The motivations for this move toward supplier rationalization are based not only on economics and the search for continuous quality improvement and innovation, but also on a realization that there is a limit to the extent to which multiple supplier relationships can be effectively managed. As a result of these changes in the supply chain, a growing interdependency among the parties in the chain has emerged along with the realization that cooperation and partnerships are essential prerequisites for the achievement of long-term mutual benefit. Table 5.1 compares the traditional and partnership supply chain models.

Attributes	Traditional model	Partnership model
Suppliers	Multiple sources, competition	A few preferred suppliers
Nature of competition	Closed, friendly, plenty of business	Collaborative, dynamic
Basis of sourcing	Wide inquiries, lowest bid, price based	Performance history, long-term sourcing
Data and information exchange	Very restricted	Two-way, long-term
Cost sharing	Buyers take all savings; suppliers hide savings	Win-win, shared costs
Capacity management	Few problems, some poor scheduling	Coordinated and jointly planned
Delivery practices	Delayed schedules, large quantities	Small quantities, agreed-on basis, dynamic
Price changes	General negotiation, win-lose game	Economies and planned reduction, win-win situations
Attitude to quality	Inspection based	Joint planning for product or service quality in the design, process control based
Role of research and development	One sided, either assembler or supplier	Shared

Table 5.1 Comparison of traditional vs. partnership model.

PRINCIPLES OF SUPPLIER PARTNERSHIPS

Fundamental requirements for the development of partnerships and networks are trust and common objectives among all parties. In partnerships, organizations form close and lasting ties with others in the value-added chain, with each player in the value-added chain having a stake in the others' success.

The ability to see beyond corporate boundaries has another important advantage. It permits recognition of serious threats that lie elsewhere along the value-added chain. Strategic partnering is an ongoing, long-term relationship with common organizational goals for a longer period. It is a way to deliver value to customers and profitability partners under the umbrella of memoranda of understanding and subsequent contracts. These can include but are not limited to common study of customer requirements for designing tailor-made solutions, transferring of technology, and setting up distribution networks.

Operational partnering is an as-needed, shorter-term relationship for obtaining parity with competitors. There is no easy answer to the question about what makes a relationship a partnership. A common suggestion is that a partnership is a close relationship. To give meaning to a close relationship, you have to consider the degree of integration between the buying and the selling organizations. Focusing on integration is an important step toward a better understanding of the critical dimensions of supplier relationships.

Cross-functional teams comprising representatives from different functions such as design, manufacturing, quality, engineering, operations, service, finance, and information technology from both customer and partner suppliers are a foundation of partnerships. Synergy, input from all functions, time compression, and overcoming organizational resistance are the benefits of the cross-functional teams. Executive sponsorship and having effective and qualified members are prerequisites for achieving these benefits.

Involvement of preferred suppliers such as partners in new product development has several benefits. This is in accordance with the quality management philosophy of incorporating quality from conception through design, requirement analysis, development, production, and change management. Specifications and standardizations are primary needs in the requirements documents and usually are defined as the acceptance criteria. There are forums and organizations that define and standardize these specifications and standards. Suppliers and customers join these platforms to participate and influence in these processes.

In earlier chapters we discussed examples of industry, government, national, and international management standards such as ISO 9001 or those by ANSI or ASTM. Process and product standards are much too numerous to list.

WORKING OUT PARTNERSHIPS AND COLLABORATION

Walter A. Shewhart's plan-do-check-act (PDCA) cycle, which is a well-known continuous improvement method, may be employed for a partnership model. Figure 5.1 is a generic PDCA model that can be used to work out partnership and customer–supplier collaborations.

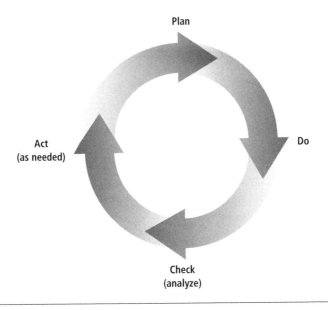

Figure 5.1 PDCA cycle.

The plan stage for sourcing consists of a basic analysis and starts with a spend analysis and diagnosis of the value being purchased. Other plan areas are supplier segmentation and selection of suitable suppliers for different commodities.

In the do stage, supply chain management program development and procurement activities should be started with a few selected suppliers.

During the check stage, results of the SCM development programs are evaluated. Different tools such as benchmarking and supplier scorecards are used. Specific projects are assigned to different suppliers, and the results of these activities are evaluated.

The last part of the cycle, the act stage, is when the projects with promising results are standardized and extended to all other suppliers.

KEY FACTORS IN PARTNERSHIPS

Partnership relations have challenges and obstacles to overcome. Following are the key success factors:

- Partnership consolidation
- Long-term commitments
- Highly integrated operations
- Frequent, planned communication
- Mutual trust and integrity

- Understanding of cross cultures
- Open communications
- Confidentiality
- System approach
- Quality management
- Shared cost savings
- An understanding of the total value chain economics for the product
- An analytic process, which systematically identifies and documents untapped potential
- Senior management leadership and continuous support
- A multifunctional task force with representation of customer and supplier
- Clear understanding of the process steps leading to sustainable value
- A structure to perpetuate the partnership and future improvement

FORMAL DISPUTE RESOLUTION

Disputes about contractual issues sometimes arise between customer and supplier. Dispute resolution mechanisms fall into two types:

1. Adjudicative processes, in which a judge or arbitrator determines the outcome. These processes include litigation and arbitration.

2. Consensual processes, in which parties attempt to reach agreement. These include mediation, conciliation, negotiation, and online dispute resolution.

Litigation

The conducting of a lawsuit is called litigation. A lawsuit is a criminal or civil action brought before a court in which the plaintiff seeks a legal remedy. Defendants are required to answer the plaintiff's complaint. If the plaintiff is successful, judgment will be given in the plaintiff's favor and a range of court orders may be issued to enforce a right, impose a penalty or sentence, award damages, impose an injunction to prevent an act or compel an act, or obtain a declaratory judgment to prevent future legal disputes.

A lawsuit may involve dispute resolution of private law issues between individuals, business entities, or nonprofit organizations. A lawsuit may also involve public law issues in criminal cases and in those jurisdictions that enable the government to be treated as if it were a private party in a civil case, as plaintiff or defendant regarding an injury, or that provide the government with a civil cause of action to enforce certain laws rather than to criminally prosecute.

Mediation

Mediation not only functions for dispute resolution but also is a way to prevent disputes. It can be used to facilitate the process of contract negotiation by identifying mutual interests and strengthening communication between parties. Framing of a dispute is of vital importance during the course of this method. A mediator uses appropriate techniques to open and improve bilateral dialogue between parties and is viewed as impartial.

Conciliation

In conciliation, parties resolve their differences with the help of conciliator. Conciliation is similar to shuttle diplomacy as the conciliator meets parties separately and helps them reach a consensus that can be recorded as a contract with legal protection. Parties usually get together for ratification after they have developed a consensus.

Arbitration

Arbitration is a widely practiced process in which a dispute is resolved by an impartial adjudicator who is appointed by a competent court. The decision of the arbitrator is considered final and binding on both disputants and is issued as court decree. An arbitration code for civil procedure is observed, and the arbitrator may relax some of the rules in accordance with arbitration laws. Arbitration is faster than litigation, but the arbitration award has to be issued as court decree to take effect for enforcement.

Online Dispute Resolution

Online dispute resolution (ODR) uses new technologies to solve disputes. It also involves the application of traditional dispute resolution methods to disputes that arise online. ODR is time effective, cost efficient, and can overcome geographical hurdles. It requires knowledge of information technology, ODR and law, the legality of proceedings, and industry support.

INTELLECTUAL PROPERTY

The supplier's involvement in new product development invokes the need for nondisclosure and intellectual property agreements. Intellectual properties are protected by patent, copyright, and trade secret clauses in the U.S. Constitution and relevant laws. Federal patent and copyright laws overrule any contradictory state statutes. A United Nations World Intellectual Property Organization was created for protection of intellectual property rights. Rules in other countries vary and should be investigated.

PROFESSIONAL ETHICS

Professional ethics are the social codes based on widely accepted principles. ASQ has such a code for its members.[2] The Institute of Supply Management (ISM) has published professional ethics for the supply chain.[3] Additionally, organizations have their own corporate ethics policies that are used by functional departments to define their policies and guide their staff on what is acceptable and what is not.

The principles and standards of an ethical supply chain, adapted from the Institute of Supply Management's code, include are but not limited to the following:

- *Ethical perception.* Avoid the intent and appearance of unethical or compromising practice in relationships, actions, and communications.

- *Loyalty to employer.* Demonstrate loyalty to your employer by diligently following instructions of your employer, using reasonable care and only the authority granted.

- *Conflict of interest.* Refrain from any private business or professional activity that would create a conflict between personal interests and those of your employer.

- *Gratuities.* Refrain from soliciting or accepting money, loans, credits, discounts, gifts, entertainment, favors, or services from present or potential suppliers.

- *Confidentiality.* Handle confidential or proprietary information with due care and proper consideration of ethical and legal ramifications and governmental regulations.

- *Treatment of suppliers.* Promote positive supplier relationships through courtesy and impartiality.

- *Abide by the law.* Know and obey the letter and spirit of laws governing the purchasing function and remain alert to the legal ramifications of purchasing decisions.

- *Equal opportunity.* Ensure that all segments of society have the opportunity to participate in government contracts.

- *Personal purchases for employees.* Discourage purchasing involvement in employer-sponsored programs of personal purchases that are not business related.

The stature of a purchasing profession can be enhanced by improving technical knowledge and adhering to a code of conduct.

References

1. "The Five Forces that Shape Strategy," *Harvard Business Review,* preview of article by Michael Porter, http://hbr.org/2008/01/the-five-competitive-forces-that-shape-strategy/ar/1.

2. ASQ Code of Ethics, http://asq.org/about-asq/who-we-are/ethics.html.

3. "Principles and Standards of Ethical Supply Management Conduct With Guidelines," *ISM Principles of Sustainability and Social Responsibility With a Guide to Adoption and Implementation,* Institute for Supply Management, www.ism.ws/index.cfm.

6

Monitor Supplier Performance

WHY PERFORMANCE MANAGEMENT FOR SUPPLIERS?

There are three key reasons to manage supplier performance:

1. Customers have limited resources for checking everything suppliers are doing for them. Incoming inspections are costly, not completely effective, and often repeat exactly what a supplier already is testing, inspecting, or verifying.

2. *Vertical integration* in business is a thing of the past. A customer relies heavily on the work of suppliers to provide services and products or product components that allow the customer to succeed. Suppliers are often an extension of the customer organization's business and, as such, should be evaluated on process performance. The customer organization analyzes its own processes and should also provide performance feedback to its suppliers.

3. The ISO 9000 family of quality management system (QMS) standards requires customers to evaluate supplier performance. The QMS standard controls have proven themselves to be effective and have been implemented by over a million organizations. To maintain compliance, the organization needs to implement a process for supplier evaluations and to review that process for its effectiveness.

ISO 9001 requires that the organization ensure control of processes and that this control be defined in the quality management system (QMS). The standard also requires that the organization evaluate and select suppliers, keep records of the evaluations, and verify product and services. Later in the measurement section of the standard there are requirements for control of nonconforming product, including any outsourced products. The requirements to monitor and measure point to the need for supplier performance management. Similar requirements are also found in other International Organization for Standardization (ISO) sector-specific standards to which an organization may achieve certification.

VERIFICATION OF ORDERED ITEMS

All ordered items should be inspected by the supplier at its premises, and its inspection certificates should be submitted upon the customer organization's request. When a contract or purchase order requires supplier inspections and tests to be witnessed, the customer sends an inspector to the supplier premises to verify the product conforms to requirements. This is called source inspection. It is the responsibility of suppliers to carry out final inspection regardless of product size, weight, cost, or hazard or risk issues. For important components or equipment, the customer organization may need to witness the testing and inspection process at the source.

Another variation of source inspection is to request pre-shipment samples of a lot or batch to test prior to release from the supplier's premises. This variation can be used for assessment for qualification but is not recommended for ongoing ordinary purchasing because suppliers tend to send only good samples that have already been validation tested.

Purchasing should be based on total value rather than just initial price. A supplier with the lowest quoted price may not present the lowest cost to the customer if defect costs and other risks are considered.

A control feature used to ensure conformance to the procurement requirements is receiving inspection of the supplier's product and review of supplier's documentation. The customer organization may employ additional controls such as *statistical process control (SPC)* and access to supplier data to minimize receiving and inspection costs. Details should be in some type of receiving inspection procedure. The receiving inspection may be by sampling based on the past experience with the product in question.

On receipt of material, the receiving inspector should inspect the material and review the documentation, such as material test or final inspection reports, against the requirements of the purchase order. Some items may be accepted dock-to-stock. When required, risk-based sampling plans should be used. Sampling specifications and requirements (such as *acceptance sampling*) should be in the receiving inspection program or instructions for each order. Inspectors, both internal and external, must be competent. Required competencies and individual certifications should be stipulated.

All items should be checked for:

- Appearance by visual inspection
- Quantity by comparing to shipping documents or shipping notices
- Correct markings and labeling

In most cases, product characteristics or performance are verified by test or certificate of conformance. Product characteristics include: dimensions, assay, concentration, viscosity, hardness, and so on. Product performance may be RPMs, motion, time, capacity, speed, and so on.

Even for those items inspected at their source, some degree of receiving inspection is necessary because there is the possibility the product was damaged during transport or that the wrong product was shipped.

Either for products or services, the items for receiving inspection should be defined prior to inspection, based on the past quality history.

WHAT PERFORMANCE SHOULD BE EVALUATED?

A needs analysis can help a customer determine what types of items should be included in a supplier performance feedback process. The supply, procurement, or purchasing manager and quality manager are usually tasked with developing supplier performance evaluations.

A needs analysis begins with understanding the key drivers of success for an organization by asking what performance measurements are important to the operations function. These can often be inferred from the strategic goals of the company. If a goal is to minimize inventory, for example, delivery performance for suppliers becomes a key need. If a key requirement is that supplied product meets strict regulatory tests, the supplier's ability to deliver a certificate of compliance becomes a key need.

In determining metrics, it is important to realize that right metrics drive right behavior and wrong metrics drive wrong behavior. For example, if an organization wants to encourage problem solving, it should not count the number of open problems and treat that metric as something to be reduced or avoided. Rather it should use metrics focused on the product or service (for example, scrap, waste, yield, defects per million opportunities, returns, warranty claims, and potential causes of problems). That way, problem identification will not be avoided but will be surfaced so improvements can be made.

The managers in charge of purchasing and quality should also interview senior management to learn what needs each executive might have for the suppliers. One important consideration is the ability of the supplier to control its costs so the prices it charges do not suddenly increase and have an effect on profitability. Another potential performance issue is whether the supplier tested, practiced or demonstrated that their disaster recovery plans would be effective.

The quality function could have unique requirements for suppliers that would affect performance evaluations. If a product or service provided by a supplier is found to be nonconforming, quality personnel would want to know that suppliers could evaluate that issue and define a *corrective action* that would prevent recurrence. Quality personnel would also want to know that the supplier could do trend analysis of data to identify opportunities to prevent potential nonconformities.

The design and technical functions should also be included in a needs analysis. Supply chain needs are often driven by specifications produced by either of these organizational functions. The supplier chosen must be able to meet the specification requirements, such as a C_{pK} minimum on the supplied product or components. A supplier may also be subject to regulatory requirements that could be spelled out in the specification. If a supplier needs to achieve and maintain an accreditation, certification, or regulatory mark such as that of Underwriters Laboratories (UL) or the Canadian Standards Association (CSA), the customer has to know the supplier is capable.

A needs analysis might be conducted with each unique function at an organization. The extent of the needs analysis would have to be determined by purchasing and quality. These are typical questions that would be asked during a needs analysis:

- What basic expectations for performance should we place on suppliers of products and services we use to produce products and services for our customers?

- Are there any unique supplier requirements that would come from your function here at our organization?

- Do we need to require suppliers to meet any kind of regulatory requirements or maintain any type of accreditation or certification?

- Do you currently have a method for measuring supplier performance criteria?

Monitoring Supplier Performance

Figure 6.1 illustrates a continuum of practices to monitor supplier performance. Performance monitoring begins at the individual product or service level with practices such as source inspection or 100% receiving inspection, and progresses to systems practices such as report cards and supplier certification programs. Supplier monitoring usually

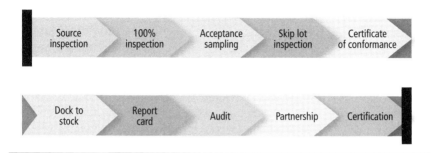

Figure 6.1 A continuum of monitoring actions.

encompasses multiple activities along this continuum and will change as organization needs dictate or as the relationships with suppliers change.

It is sometimes difficult to effectively manage all the options for monitoring supplier performance. Key considerations should include availability of people and technology to facilitate the monitoring, the budget for conducting the monitoring, and the sophistication of the supplier.

If there is a large pool of people resources and budgets for monitoring performance, an organization can typically invest in each of these monitoring activities and create a broad and effective subsystem to monitor suppliers:

- One group of resources for different types of inspections.

- Another group to work with suppliers to evaluate product and delivery performance data to allow for dock-to-stock programs.

- Still other resources to focus on creating feedback using reports cards that specify delivery, quality, and cost metrics.

- Another group to go on site visits, prepare audit reports, and work on partnerships with key suppliers.

The culmination of the continuum is when the customer can create a series of benchmarks that suppliers must meet to achieve a certified status and then certify suppliers that have met those benchmarks.

If there are limited internal people resources and budgets for monitoring performance, an organization will do well to focus its efforts on report cards and in-person audits. Business management software can be used to monitor supplier performance. It is often a simple exercise to export delivery, quality, and cost data and prepare monthly or quarterly reports by supplier. These can be e-mailed to the supply chain and discussed during audits or even over the phone.

A common first step in performance management is to ask the supplier to complete a quality management system (QMS) and organizational practices inventory. This is often called a supplier survey or supplier assessment. The assessment can be completed by the supplier and returned to the customer organization, or the assessment can include a site audit by the customer. The accuracy of the self-assessment is dependent on the competency of the person completing the assessment. It is important to also conduct as many supplier audits as possible within budgetary requirements. Site audits can help determine the suppliers' capabilities, capacities, and types of products or services provided.

ELEMENTS OF A SUPPLIER MANAGEMENT PROCESS

Supplier management should begin with segmentation of the supply chain. There are many ways to segment the supply chain, including ranking suppliers by inventory analysis, by monies spent per year, or by importance of the supplier to the products or services supplied by the customer. The purchasing or procurement function is usually tasked with this segmentation. Whatever method is chosen, it is important to document the method in a procedure that can be used to standardize the segmentation process. Figure 6.2 provides a flow of elements in a progressive supplier management process.

Once the segmentation is done, the quality representative should form a cross-functional team that has representation from departments in the company that have a stake in a supplier management process. This might include operations, purchasing, engineering, and sales. The supply purchasing or procurement department could take the lead for this team. This team should determine the metrics that can be readily generated from sources of supplier performance data and determine what kind of feedback should be given to suppliers. Feedback options include formal supplier report cards submitted to the supplier's senior management, e-mailing performance data to a buyer, or even holding an annual suppliers' conference and giving out awards for performance excellence.

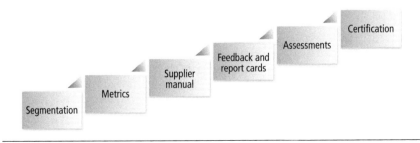

Figure 6.2 Flow of supplier management process elements.

This team should also prepare a supplier handbook or manual that will help suppliers know the unique needs and expectations for doing business with the customer organization. The handbook would provide details regarding topics ranging from how to acknowledge a purchase order to how to host an audit by the customer's quality representative. Details about supplier performance feedback methods should also be written in this manual (see Table 6.1 for an example handbook table of contents). Other feedback methods could include instructions for completing corrective action requests, how to submit first-article inspections or product warrants, how to submit product capability or reliability data, and how to submit quotes for work. The handbook is a critical step because it documents what the suppliers need to do to be successful.

Typical data needed for supplier performance could be delivery, quality level, cost control and reductions, ease of doing business, and innovation. Care should be exercised to make certain the data are free of bias that would affect a decision. Most data collected provide performance results related to delivery and quality level (percentage parts per million defective or similar). Once the data sources are determined, the team should test the data collection methods to assure the data can be collected and processed in a timely and accurate manner.

Most data collection outputs are documented as supplier report cards (see Table 6.2) that are processed and reviewed monthly by management.

Section title	Section description of contents
Section 0	1. Letter of interest from the customer organization to notify supplier of desire to approve an organization relationship after the supplier survey has been completed, submitted, and approved 2. Purchasing approval process policy 3. Supplier feedback policy for purposes of re-evaluation
Section 1	1. Supplier report card template 2. Nondisclosure agreement 3. Other regulatory agreements (as necessary)
Section 2	1. General organization background 2. Contacts 3. Organizational capabilities 4. Regulatory compliance
Section 3	QMS description and evidence requests
Section 4	Customer organization review, comments, and status (whether approved or not)

Table 6.1 Supplier quality manual and survey table of contents.

Formal reports are sent each quarter to the affected suppliers. Methods for accessing report cards can vary widely and each organization creates its own formats for providing the feedback. Suppliers that receive unsatisfactory ratings should expect to receive notifications of probationary periods during which they are expected to resolve issues to the satisfaction of the customer. If the improvement is not completed satisfactorily, the supplier should expect to be replaced.

Rating period	Total deliveries	Number on time	Number early	Number late	Number accepted	Number rejected	Delivery performance %	Quality performance %	Total score %	Quality rating	Delivery rating	Total rating
1st Qtr	178	141		37	177	1	79.2	99.4	89.3	A	C	B
2nd Qtr	136	134		2	135	1	98.5	99.3	98.9	A	B	B
3rd Qtr	136	125		11	136	0	91.9	100.0	96.0	A	B	B
4th Qtr	122	110		12	121	1	90.2	99.2	94.7	A	B	B
YTD Total	572	510	0	62	569	3	89.2	99.5	94.3	A	B	B

Scoring key: A = Excellent   B = Acceptable   C = Marginal (improvement desired)
                     D = Unacceptable (improvement required)   F = Decertify

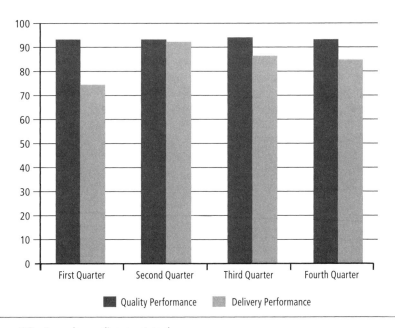

Figure 6.3   Example supplier report card.

While suppliers appreciate report cards, this should not be the only mechanism for providing feedback. A focus on building relationships with suppliers on the part of quality engineers can have an immediate payback to the organization. Supplier quality engineers (SQE) can help suppliers understand how to meet the requirements of a purchase orders and the content of a supplier quality manual. SQEs can conduct in-person audits to a defined schedule. SQEs have specialized training and education that allow them to assist with capability studies and other product and process analytics. An SQE can be a very effective technical liaison for the organization. An SQE usually has an engineering or quality degree and may be an ASQ Certified Quality Engineer.

When suppliers have problems with providing conforming processes, products, or services, the corrective action process can help the organization document the problems and provide an avenue for the supplier to respond with action plans to prevent recurrence. SQEs and purchasing professionals can help build the relationship with a supplier to a point at which actions can be taken to prevent the occurrence of potential nonconforming goods and services.

Suppliers can also be monitored remotely using software and websites. For example, suppliers submit testing results and other product analyses to an online database hosted by the customer organization. The organization could also post supplier report cards and other feedback. Corrective action requests could use this same electronic interface. The organization would have to develop necessary permissions and security controls. It is also possible for supplier audits to be conducted remotely using a service that allows two-way voice and video communication.

Partnerships with suppliers can lead to supplier certification and awards programs. A certification process has these five major steps:

1. Developing the certification process flow and requirements for achievement

2. Identifying segmented groups where certification would be useful

3. Evaluating the chosen suppliers against the achievement requirements

4. Reporting results and awarding certifications

5. Continuing monitoring to maintain status

Supplier certifications and awards programs have some expenses associated with them. Care should be exercised in all major steps of the process to minimize bias and to make certain the return on the investment makes good business sense. The certification should lead to a better partnership with the supplier, and not just be a reason to hold a gathering and give awards.

BEST PRACTICES

The five best practices listed here offer a balanced approach that can be implemented by organizations that value their supply chain relationships and have a long-term focus on success. These practices require people and monetary investments, but provide a quick return on investment:

1. Segment the supply chain so the remaining four best practices are used on those suppliers with the most strategic impact on the organization's success.

2. Conduct site visits using qualified SQEs to determine QMS and product capabilities.

3. Use site visits to collect data used to consolidate the supply chain. Many suppliers have abilities unknown to purchasing and engineering (technical) functions in the organization. Buying more products or services from the same supplier creates a better negotiating position.

4. Create partnerships with key suppliers in the supply chain. These partners are involved in all aspects of the organization's product or service life cycle and are invited to add value to those products or services.

5. Certify suppliers that achieve partner status. Certified suppliers become an extension of your organization. Certification means the supplier is good enough to be part of your organization. Resources then are not used to inspect products and micromanage the supplier.

7

Supply Chain Management Processes

SUPPLY CHAIN DEFINED BY THE EXPERTS

The global economy has been both a challenge and an opportunity for organizations to manage their supply chains. To manage them efficiently, we must first agree on the definition of "supply chain" and then understand all of its components.

The Council of Supply Chain Management Professionals (CSCMP) defines a supply chain as encompassing "the planning and management of all activities involved in sourcing, procurement, conversion, and logistics management. It also includes the crucial components of coordination and collaboration with channel partners, which can be suppliers, intermediaries, third-party service providers and customers."[1]

This broad view of supply chain and logistics management includes a variety of organizational functions, some of which are not always openly stated. These include:

- *Information management.* Includes generating and sharing customer, forecasting, production, and all other information required to ensure that supply matches demand throughout the supply chain.

- *Procurement.* The acquisition of goods or services, which may include functions beyond the purchase such as expediting, transportation, and quality.

- *Quality.* Responsible for the evaluation and qualification of potential suppliers and the reevaluation of existing suppliers to help ensure the suppliers' systems and processes are capable of supplying goods and services to predetermined specifications.

- *Inventory flow scheduling and control.* Responsibility for the accuracy, timeliness, and management of maintenance repairs and operations, raw material, work-in-process, and finished goods inventory.

- *Transportation systems operation and infrastructure.* The efficient movement of material and goods throughout the supply chain.

- *Distribution facilities management.* Storage of goods until needed by the customer (or manufacturer in the case of raw materials and products or components).

- *Customer service.* Includes order management and fulfillment, and assisting the customer throughout the order process.[2]

THE SCOR MODEL

The Supply Chain Operations Reference (SCOR) model[3] is a common-sense way of defining, understanding, measuring, and improving the various supply chain processes. It applies to all organizations, be they for-profit, non-profit, government, or non-government. The SCOR model is based on five general management processes: plan, source, make, deliver, and return. Following is a brief description of each (as shown in Figure 7.1):

- *Plan.* Processes that balance aggregate demand and supply to develop a course of action that best meets sourcing, production, and delivery requirements.

- *Source.* Processes that procure goods and services to meet planned or actual demand.

- *Make.* Processes that transform product or service to a finished state to meet planned or actual demand.

- *Deliver.* Processes that provide finished goods and services to meet planned or actual demand, typically including order management, transportation management, and distribution management.

- *Return.* Processes associated with returning or receiving returned products for any reason. (Services cannot be returned, but they can be repeated.) These processes extend into post-delivery customer support.

The supply chain, when considered in this way, is actually more like a supply web, because an organization has a complex network of customers, distributors, wholesalers, suppliers, and sub-suppliers that may include logistics, transportation, manufacturing, warehousing, and other services.

Some even refer to the downstream processes (toward the customers) as the demand chain and the upstream processes (toward the suppliers) as the supply chain. In any case, the SCOR model helps make sense of the complexities of the supply chain and to define and manage it.

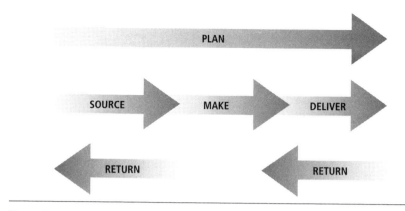

Figure 7.1 SCOR model.

PLAN

In many ways, the planning process is most important, as it can ultimately determine the success or failure of the entire supply chain process. There are many aspects to this process, and the use of technology has had a major influence on collaboration and visibility with supply chain partners, both downstream and upstream. Planning can help minimize what is known as "the bullwhip effect." This refers to a trend of larger and larger swings in inventory in response to changes in demand as one looks at organizations further back in the supply chain for a product. The bullwhip effect does not occur if all orders exactly meet the demand of each period, therefore it is important to extend the visibility of customer demand as far as possible.

Supply Planning

In this process, the updated forecasts are netted against current on-hand inventory balances, current work orders or purchase orders, lead times, and safety stock/time requirements to determine future purchasing or production requirements. This is known as time-phased planning.

To generate future requirements (known as planned receipts and, in cases when supply lead time is backed off, planned orders), it is usually best (in the case of finished goods) to calculate economic order quantities (EOQ) to answer the "how much" part of the question. The EOQ is a calculation that attempts to find an order quantity that minimizes total costs. This is the point at which holding or carrying costs and ordering or setup costs intersect.

Holding costs for inventory include capital, taxes, storage, insurance, and other costs that can be up to 25% or more of the cost of the item annually. Thus the continuing pressure is to keep inventory at a minimum.

Ordering or setup costs are the costs associated with either placing an order or performing a changeover of a machine. The tradeoff is that more frequent orders or changeovers mean you can order in smaller quantities, thus lowering holding costs but possibly raising ordering costs, including those for freight. The idea is to try to minimize the time and cost of changeovers or ordering so they are not obstacles to smaller batch sizes, which will lower overall average inventory levels.

Next, we need to answer the "when" question (when to order). This is typically done using either a reorder point or reorder time model. Reorder point takes into account replenishment lead time and daily demand to determine when to order. Reorder time looks instead at days-of-supply targets of items to determine when to order.

The net requirements from this process are then aggregated, and any capacity issues are identified and addressed at that point in a series of meetings, typically with manufacturing and purchasing involved.

Supply planning may also apply to service organizations that order and store material or equipment used to perform the service such as installers.

Planning Technology

A family of software known as advanced planning and scheduling (APS) is used in this process to generate aggregate plans as well as more detailed master production schedules (MPS) that will drive actual production or purchasing requirements. In many cases, purchasing requirements for raw materials and components come from material requirements planning (MRP) systems, which are time-phased systems that extrapolate finished good requirements from the MPS into raw and component needs.

Once various parties have agreed to the supply plan, there should be an executive meeting to finalize plans for the near term.

SOURCING

Sourcing refers to a number of procurement practices that are aimed at finding, evaluating, and engaging suppliers of goods and services. The purchasing function sources inputs into the transformational process of an organization. These inputs range from tangible products (for example, raw materials, parts, and capital equipment) to services such as, employee travel, healthcare, and consulting.

The purchasing cycle describes the tasks required. It starts with the purchasing function's receiving user requirements that are very specific and detail the product or service characteristics. Once these requirements or specifications have been clarified, a make-or-buy decision must be made. If the product or service can't be delivered internally, then purchasing must identify and evaluate potential suppliers. This usually starts with a *request for information (RFI)*, which leads to a request for proposal (RFP) or request for quote (RFQ), when a supplier is selected and a contract is agreed to along with order details. Finally, steps must be taken to monitor and manage the relationship with the supplier.

There is an increased need for global sourcing whereby suppliers can be in any geographic region. The process is similar but is more complex because issues such as language, currency, customs, tariffs, duties, and long lead times must be considered.[4]

Sourcing Technology

A variety of technology is available for this function. It can range from modules of *enterprise resource planning (ERP)* systems that generate purchase orders from an MRP system, to electronic data interchange for the electronic exchange of information between organizations, and eventually to e-procurement, including electronic catalogs, exchanges, and auctions.

MAKE

The actual transformation of inputs (for example, raw materials) into outputs (for example, finished goods or services) might not be considered by many to be a supply chain function, but without the function, there would be nothing to manufacture.

Make Processes

Most organizations use one of the following make processes:

- *Process focus.* Highly customized, low volume. Often referred to as a job or batch process products (for example, printing service store).

- *Repetitive focus.* Assembly line process. Less flexible but more volume than a process focus (for example, automobile manufacturing).

- *Product focus.* Often referred to as a continuous process. Generally has high volume but low variety (for example, chemical or food and beverage plants).

- *Mass customization.* High volume items are made to order (for example, computers).

Make Strategies

The production and inventory strategies are typically performed in one of the following ways:

- *Make-to-stock.* Finished goods are produced to a forecast and produced in batches. They are kept in stock and available for immediate delivery. This is common in manufacturing, education, and process industries.

- *Make-to-order.* Items are made to customer specifications in low volumes, sometimes in units of one. This is common in government and health care sectors.

- *Engineer–to-order.* Customer item specifications require unique engineering or customization. This type of order typically has significant customer involvement. An organization may require a very specialized piece of equipment or service.

- *Assemble-to-order.* Entails making a large number of products from relatively few subassemblies or components. The concepts of postponement (kitting or assembling when the order is received) and customization can be executed with this method to help make the supply chain more efficient. Mail and Internet ordering use this approach.

Make Technology

Technology used in the make function can be sophisticated in order to generate optimal schedules. Short-term scheduling can range from simple Gantt charts (a sideways bar chart) to very sophisticated finite capacity scheduling systems, a scheduling method that matches resource requirements to a finite supply of available resources to develop a realistic production plan.

DELIVERY AND WAREHOUSING

Delivery generally includes the transportation and distribution function or supply and demand chain. In many cases, this is an area that is frequently outsourced as it may not be a core competency of an organization. Many companies may outsource transportation services (common carriers or small package delivery), warehousing (public warehousing, cold storage), and even third-party logistics services (transportation, warehousing, data storage, Internet connections, and value-added services such as kitting and light manufacturing or assembly).

Warehousing

A warehouse or distribution center is a building for the storage and subsequent distribution of goods. It may also be the place where services are provided, such as a hospital or college campus. The objective of warehouse layout is to find the optimum trade-off between material handling cost and costs associated with warehouse space, so it is important to maximize the cube, or full volume, of the facility. Typically, the number of different items stocked has an inverse relationship to maximizing the cube. Think of the extreme of only one type of item in a warehouse. They are all the same size, so the cube is maximized.

> In the past we have not always reviewed our warehouse and transportation needs properly. We did not consider the size of the product, the size of the container, pallet, or boxes, and returnable packaging or safety stock needs. In some cases, inadequate packaging or poor packaging design has required more storage space to avoid product damage.

Travel time is critical to warehouse operator productivity, so layout has a direct effect on this and must always be considered.

Because warehouses are subject to frequent outsourcing, a break-even analysis should be performed to see whether a particular volume justifies building an organization's own warehouse.

Warehousing Technology

Warehousing uses a variety of technologies. Warehouse management systems are a class of software that helps to manage within the four walls of the warehouse. Other technology used includes radio frequency bar code scanning, radio frequency identification (RFID), *pick to light,* and automated storage and retrieval systems.

Transportation

There are various modes of transportation, each with its own characteristics. In general they are:

- *Trucking.* Most manufactured goods move by truck. It is a flexible form of transportation with relatively short transit times. In general, the cost for a full truck (truckload or TL) is less per hundredweight than shipping smaller loads (less than truckload or LTL).

- *Railroads.* Railroads typically offer the lowest cost of transportation but are much slower, so they typically carry heavy, bulky cargo such as coal and salt. The advent of containerization has made intermodal transportation popular (containers that go from trucks or ships to rail and back to truck).

- *Air freight.* This is the premium form of transportation and the fastest. It is generally used for small, light, and higher-value packages.

- *Waterways.* This is the oldest form of transportation and domestically used more for raw material transport. Internationally, a majority of cargo comes from Asia on ships loaded with containers (like trucking, but called "container load and less than container load" with different rate structures).

- *Pipeline.* Specifically for gas, oil, and other liquids.
- *Internet.* For delivery of data.

No matter the mode of transportation, action must be taken to avoid loss or damage to the product, material, or information.

Each of these modes is subject to outsourcing. In some cases such as product storage conditions, it might make sense for an organization to have its own fleet of trucks; in other cases, not. Which mode to choose depends on doing a cost of shipping alternatives analysis in which the costs and service trade-offs of the various modes considered are looked at. The general concept is to see whether the reduced transit time of a premium mode (for example, less pipeline inventory and thus less carrying cost) justifies the increased cost of its transportation service.

Transportation Technology

Transportation management systems are a breed of software that helps to increase visibility into a supply chain. This type of software may be part of a larger ERP system. It may include functions such as tracking, tracing, costing and carrier selection, and management.

RETURNS

Reverse logistics is the process of the return and reuse, disposal or repair of products and materials. When this is integrated into a supply chain, it is referred to as a closed-loop process. This process is quite different from forward logistics flow. It's necessary to have convenient and efficient collection points as well as a clear process for return authorization. Companies often issue a return merchandise authorization.

There are many routes that returns can take depending on whether they will be repaired and returned, cleaned and refurbished, disassembled and recycled or safe disposal. It is important that waste is properly disposed of and product information communicated so as to make future improvements in the product.[5]

Return Technology

Reverse logistics, such as product returns, has always been important to manufacturers and retailers, but until recently this process has gotten little respect from high-level executives. Not too long ago, software specifically designed for supporting the process didn't exist, which left organizations with the choice of developing their own systems, building reverse-logistics capabilities into existing systems, or using third-party service providers such as Federal Express to manage it. Now, several software companies have developed off-the-shelf applications to help manage this process.

MEASURING SUPPLY CHAIN PERFORMANCE

You can't improve something if you don't measure it. This saying is never truer than when determining the performance of your supply chain and logistics function.

The first step is determining which measurements are important to your organization. The measurements should support your organization's overall strategy and should be unique to each process. The next step is to benchmark your practices against desired practices to see where they stand against best practices as well as your targets.

The SCOR model looks at measuring the performance of the supply chain and comparing it to internal and external industry goals. Supply chain performance is focused on:

- *Delivery reliability.* Achievement of customer demand fulfillment on time, completely, without damage, and so on.

- *Responsiveness.* The time it takes to react to and fulfill customer demand.

- *Flexibility.* The ability of the supply chain to respond to increased or decreased demand within a given planned period.

- *Cost.* Objective assessment of all components of supply chain expenses.

- *Asset management.* The assessment of all resources used to fulfill customer demand.

Table 7.1 illustrates some sample performance measurements based on the SCOR Model.

Performance attributes and associated level 1 metrics, SCOR, version 6.0.

Performance attribute	Performance attribute definition	SCOR level 1 metric
Delivery reliability	Supply chain performance in delivering: • the correct product • to the correct place and the correct customer • at the correct time • in perfect condition and packaging • in the correct quantity • with the correct documentation	• Delivery performance • Fill rate • Perfect order fulfillment
Responsiveness	How quickly a supply chain delivers products to the customer	• Order fulfillment lead time

(continued)

Table 7.1 SCOR model performance attributes.

Source: Supply Chain Council, www.supply-chain.org (accessed 2012).

Performance attribute	Performance attribute definition	SCOR level 1 metric
Flexibility	How quickly a supply chain responds to marketplace changes; agility in gaining or maintaining a competitive edge.	• Supply chain response time • Production flexibility
Cost	The costs associated with operating the supply chain.	• Cost of goods sold • Total supply chain management cost • Value-added productivity • Warranty/returns processing cost
Asset management	How effectively a company manages assets to satisfy demand. Includes fixed assets and working capital.	• Cash-to-cash cycle time • Inventory days of supply • Asset turns

Table 7.1 SCOR model performance attributes.
Source: Supply Chain Council, www.supply-chain.org (accessed 2012).

Another way to look at performance measurement is by using the following three categories:[6]

1. **Customer relationship**
   - Percentage of orders taken accurately
   - Time to complete the order placement process
   - Customer satisfaction with the order placement process
   - Customer's evaluation of firm's environmental stewardship

2. **Order fulfillment**
   - Percentage of incomplete orders shipped
   - Percentage of orders shipped on time
   - Time to fulfill the order
   - Percentage of botched services or returned items
   - Cost to produce the service or item
   - Customer satisfaction with the order fulfillment process
   - Inventory levels of work-in-process and finished goods
   - Amount of greenhouse gasses emitted into the air

3. **Supplier relationship**
   - Percentage of suppliers' deliveries on time
   - Suppliers' lead times
   - Percentage of defects in services and purchased materials
   - Cost of services and purchased materials
   - Inventory levels of supplies and purchased components
   - Evaluation of suppliers' collaboration on streamlining and waste conversion
   - Amount of transfer of environmental technologies to suppliers
   - Corrective actions and effectiveness of actions taken

In the end, which metrics are appropriate to their organization and what the actual targets should be is up to the individual organization.

Measurement Technology

Most of the technology previously mentioned has the capability to capture and display these various supply chain metrics. Additionally, the concept of data analytics, which has been around for about 10 years and is the science of examining raw data for the purpose of drawing conclusions about the information, has led to a new category of software called supply chain analytics. Supply chain analytics combines technology with human insight to identify trends, perform comparisons, and identify opportunities in a supply chain.

RISK MANAGEMENT

Risk management (see glossary definition) is an important aspect of supply chain management planning. Several industries, such as aerospace with the AS9100 standard, automotive with ISO/TS 16949, shipping with ISO 28000, and medical devices with ISO 13485, have recognized the importance of risk management.

Risk management is a necessary tool for effective project management. There are many situations when project management should be used to identify, control, and monitor risk. With regard to a supply chain, project management and risk management go hand in hand. Some example activities of when project management and risk management would be beneficial are:

- *Selection of a new supplier.* Performing an organizational risk evaluation to determine supplier's capabilities and feasibility.

- *Management of obsolescence* (see Appendix A). Monitoring if and when certain products, materials, or processes can be discontinued.

- *Introduction of new products.* Initial determination of design requirements, procurement sources of materials, and use of lessons learned from previous designs.
- *Transfer of work.* From internal to external or from one supplier to another.

Example objectives of the risk management process include:

- Early detection of weak points during contracts, in design, development, processes, and during procurement
- Definition of possible failure causes and effects, and assignment of appropriate mitigation and contingency actions
- Identification of opportunities to improve quality and reliability of product during production
- Implementation of corrective and preventive actions before the start of production
- Reduction of future costs as a result of proactive implementation of preventive actions rather than reactive corrective actions or failure analysis
- Improvement of the reliability of a product before the start of production

The risk management process includes planning, identification, analysis, responses, and monitoring and control of a project. The objectives of risk management are to increase the probability and effect of positive events and to decrease the probably and effect of adverse events. Risk management processes (see Figure 7.2) include the following:

- *Risk management planning.* Deciding how to approach, plan, and execute the risk management activities for a project.
- *Risk identification.* Determining which risks might affect the project and documenting their characteristics.
- *Risk analysis.* Evaluating the probability of occurrence and the consequences of that occurrence.
- *Risk response planning.* Developing options and actions to enhance opportunities and reduce (mitigate) threats to objectives. Risk can be accepted, transferred to others (through insurance), or controlled.
- *Risk monitoring and improvement.* Tracking identified risks, monitoring residual risks, identifying new risks, executing risk response plans, and evaluating their effectiveness throughout the project life cycle.

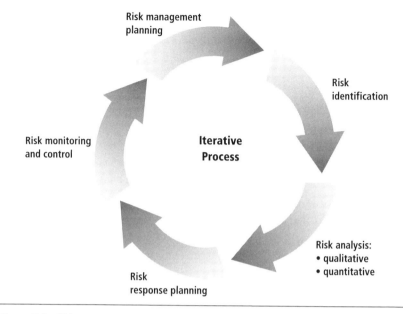

Figure 7.2 Risk management process.

The processes interact with each other. Each process can involve participation of one or more people or groups of people based on the needs, size, and complexity of the organization and/or project.

The organization should have a consistent approach to risk that will meet its requirements. Communication about risk and its handling should be open and honest. Risk responses must reflect an organization's perceived balance between risk taking and risk avoidance. The organization should be committed to addressing the management of risk proactively and consistently. In addition, the organization should be proactive in recognizing needs and opportunities for the application of risk management to all aspects of supply chain management. Risk can come from external sources, which are outside of the organization's control. Risk can also come from internal sources and be within the control of the organization.

Areas to consider for potential risk are:

- Project management, such as schedule, scope, and cost

- Manufacturing, including capacity, capability, facilities, equipment, and special processes

- Commercial matters such as exchange rates, markets, and exporting requirements

- Technical and design issues such as new technologies, obsolescence, design capabilities, and capacities
- Customer issues such as requirements, stability, and relationships
- Financial matters such as contracts, debt, taxes, and capital
- Supply chain matters such as transportation, first-article inspections, monitoring, performance, and requirements flow down
- Environmental issues such as legislation, climate, safety, and natural disasters
- External issues such as regulatory, political, geographic location, and international trafficking in arms regulations
- Human resources including availability of skills, educational levels, and language
- Sourcing options such as sole source or internal sources compared to multiple sources

Every organization today faces greater and greater uncertainty due to such challenges as global economics, politics, environmental concerns, and changing requirements from legislation and regulation. An important strategy for every organization is to be proactive by anticipating and addressing risks before they occur. For a supply chain, risk management has definite advantages as a planning tool for new supplier selection, new product introduction, transfer of work, obsolescence management, and changes to production processing, materials, or location.

References and Notes

1. www.cscmp.org (accessed 2012).
2. Paul A. Myerson, *Lean Supply Chain & Logistics Management,* McGraw-Hill Professional, 2012.
3. The SCOR model is a process reference model developed by the management consulting firm PRTM and endorsed by the Supply Chain Council as the cross-industry de-facto standard diagnostic tool for supply chain management. SCOR enables users to address, improve, and communicate supply chain management practices within and between all interested parties in an extended enterprise.
4. Roger Schroeder, Susan Meyer Goldstein, and M. Johnny Rungtusanatham, *Operations Management,* fifth edition, McGraw-Hill, 2011.
5. Lee J. Krajewski, Larry P. Ritzman, and Manoj K. Malhotra, *Operations Management—Process and Supply Chains,* ninth edition, Prentice-Hall, 2010.
6. Ibid.

Appendix A

Obsolescence Management

With today's rapidly changing technology and materials, obsolescence has an increased potential to affect products and can appear at any stage of the product life cycle. Obsolescence can be defined as the loss or discontinuance of a material or process from the current source. It is no longer produced or available in the marketplace. Generally, there is no replacement available or the replacement is not retroactively compatible, such as in the case of software. Replacement might be available but due to transportation, cost, or application (intended use), it is limited or restricted. Obsolescence is inevitable and must be addressed. With proper planning and risk management, an organization can minimize its adverse effects and costs.

Electronics is an area that is very susceptible to obsolescence. As this industry continues to evolve, the life cycle of the products is being reduced because of consumer demand. Environmental requirements and regulations are also impacting the materials and processes that are available.

Regulations such as REACH and RoHS have had a major effect on the availability and reformulations of many chemicals. REACH is the European Community regulation on chemicals and their safe use that went into force on June 1, 2007. It deals with the registration, evaluation, authorization, and restriction of chemical substances. RoHS is an acronym for the European Union (EU) directive for the restriction of hazardous substances, limiting the use of six hazardous substances in the manufacture of various types of electrical and electronic equipment. It was adopted in February 2003 by the EU and took effect in July 2006; it is required to be enforced and become law in each EU member state.

Examples of regulation-driven obsolescence are the European restrictions placed on a broad array of many consumer electronics products and components such as paints and pigments, polyvinyl chloride (PVC) used on power cords and USB cables, solders with lead, printed circuit boards leads and interfaces, batteries, lamps and light bulbs. Additionally, the ban on concentrations of brominated flame retardants

(BFR) above 0.1% in plastics has had an effect on plastic recycling. Plastics with high BFR concentrations have higher handling or disposal costs, while plastics with levels below 0.1% BFR concentration have value as recyclable materials.

The U.S. Environmental Protection Agency (EPA) continues to increase regulations on emission standards for automobiles as mandated by the Clean Air Act or regulations establishing the basic structure for regulating discharges of pollutants into the waters of the United States by the Clean Water Act. As a manufacturer, reviewing and monitoring applicable government and regulatory requirements is a necessity to ensure proper product realization planning.

Obsolescence management is a proactive approach for monitoring the status of components and materials to allow sufficient time and resources to develop and implement effective solutions. Additionally, notification of customers of the end of life of their components and materials by suppliers and *processors* needs to be included as part of the obsolescence management process. Obsolescence should be managed and integrated into every aspect of the life cycle of the product, which includes concept, design, development, procurement, production, and in-service support. The primary goal of obsolescence management is to achieve cost-effective control of a product through its life cycle while ensuring ongoing availability of production materials, equipment, and processes needed to support production requirements.

The general approach to the obsolescence management process can be represented by the following five activities:

1. *Notifications of obsolescence.* Notifications may be initiated by various sources and include notifying customers and users of an upcoming discontinuance of certain materials, products, and processes from sources caused by international standards and specifications, obsolescent software program tools, industrial forums (such as the Government-Industry Data Exchange Program), and internal design requirements.

2. *Evaluating design for product life cycle.* The design process should evaluate technologies, suppliers, processes, materials, and other areas throughout the design process to ensure there is no mismatch between the component or material supply and the life of product for the industry application.

3. *Establishing design requirements.* These include an obsolescence plan, which involves risk management and contingencies for those with forecasted limited supply issues or dependencies.

4. *Identifying and selecting components to minimize obsolescence risk.*

5. *Ongoing monitoring of the obsolescence plan.*

Obsolescence planning should be performed by reviewing the availability of items that can affect the supply chain and production capability. These assessments should be done regularly at different stages of the product life cycle. Reviews should be conducted by representatives from various functions of the organization, typically including engineering, supply chain management, quality, finance, operations and planning, inventory control, and sales and marketing. Planning begins at the start of product realization and should be assessed regularly as a form of risk management by developing mitigation and contingency plans and actions when potential obsolescence of materials or processes is identified. The assessments should include evaluations of the following areas:

- Hardware (off-the-shelf product, catalog items, equipment, and standard parts)
- Software (updated versions, discontinued applications, and customized programs)
- People skills (training, education, and work experience)
- Raw materials (chemicals, coatings, and composite materials such as carbon fiber)
- Legislative and regulatory requirements (REACH, RoHS, and EPA)

If implemented and maintained, the benefits of an effective obsolescence management process are:

- Reliable availability of materials and processes for producing the product or service
- Minimization of disruption in the supply chain
- Lower design cycle time
- A robust product design process with lower potential for needing a product redesign
- Control of product cost
- Maintenance of a focus on customer satisfaction

Today's ever-changing technologies, a global economy, increasing concerns about energy resources and climate change, growing environmental awareness on the part of communities and governments, and increased awareness and knowledge about chemicals and substances that may cause health concerns have led to a recognized need for ongoing changes in consumer products and processes.

During economic downturns, many organizations are unable to sustain operations, therefore their products and materials are no longer available. To survive, some organizations consolidate and eliminate products that do not add value or profit. As technology changes rapidly, what is high-tech and a new concept today may be considered old technology and obsolete within a year or two. Televisions, cellular phones, computers, and software applications are perfect examples of how quickly obsolescence can occur.

As participants in a global economy, organizations must be informed of all the applicable regulations and laws and comply with other countries' requirements if they want to be exporters. Obsolescence management throughout the life cycle of a product is becoming a necessity. This life cycle starts with product realization (concept, design and development), continues during the production process (which includes supply chain management and production processing), and goes to the end of life of the product, when considerations must be made regarding its safe disposal.

Appendix B
Supplier Assessment Tool

DIRECTIONS FOR
AUDITOR OR ASSESSOR

1. Use this form to complete supplier assessments. Complete all sections. If a process or section does not apply, indicate this in the comments section. Explain why the process or section does not apply.

Note: This assessment form can also be used for a supplier self-assessment.

2. Explain the purpose or objectives for auditing the supplier prior to or while doing business with our organization:

   a. Verify suppliers have sound financial/fiscal performance as determined by an independent party such as Dun & Bradstreet (D&B) or a similar service.

   b. Verify supplier organizations have a quality management system (QMS) compliant to all requirements of ISO 9001 or another QMS standard.

   c. Verify supplier organizations can provide the appropriate evidence that all processes used to manufacture parts or provide services were done according to their established procedures.

   d. Verify the supplier organization has the capability to conform to customer requirements.

   e. Verify supplier organizations will provide timely responses to any nonconforming material reports.

   f. Verify supplier organizations will deliver parts on time, as specified on purchase orders.

3. Request the supplier complete a nondisclosure agreement, if one is not already on file.

4. Provide assessment results to supplier management (such as the quality manager and the materials manager).

Statement of Audit

The audit team has reviewed the quality management system and organizational practices of this supplier and recommends the following:

☐ Approve as is.　　　☐ Approve after completion of corrective action.

☐ Do not approve (provide explanation here).

_____

_____

_____

Signed by audit team leader:

Name:	Date:

A. General organization information

Contacts			
Top management: CEO/general mgr.	Name:	Phone:	
	Email:	Fax:	
Sales and marketing	Name:	Phone:	
	Email:	Fax:	
Customer service	Name:	Phone:	
	Email:	Fax:	
Engineering	Name:	Phone:	
	Email:	Fax:	
Quality	Name:	Phone:	
	Email:	Fax:	
Accounting	Name:	Phone:	
	Email:	Fax:	
	Name:	Phone:	
	Email:	Fax:	
	Name:	Phone:	
	Email:	Fax:	

Ownership? ☐ Public ☐ Private	Number of years operating:
Estimated annual revenue: $	Is the organization certified to ISO 9001 or another QMS standard? ☐ ISO 9001 ☐ Other *If yes, forward a copy of your current certificate to your customer purchasing contact. Complete A–C only.* *If no, complete all sections of the survey.*
Union or nonunion facility? ☐ Union ☐ Nonunion	If not certified to a QMS standard, do you have a quality manual or equivalent? ☐ Yes ☐ No
What percentage of your business will our organization represent? ☐ >/=20% ☐ <20%, >10% ☐ </=10%	*If yes, forward a copy of the manual to your customer purchasing contact.*
Do you now have or have you had an organizational relationship with our organization? ☐ Yes ☐ No	*If no, provide a date when it will be completed:*

B. Organization capabilities

Production lead time:	Prototype lead time:

Does your company have this capability? Check all that apply. ☐ Email ☐ EDI ☐ Bar coding ☐ Reuseable shipping containers ☐ Kanban
Kanban capabilities (describe):
What type of MRP system do you have?
Are you using lean, Six Sigma, or similar process improvement methods? ☐ Yes ☐ No
Do you utilize CAD/CAM or similar software? ☐ Yes ☐ No

Total facility square footage:	Type of building:

What percentage of our business would be your business?
Describe the primary product families the supplier organization produces:

Engineering capabilities
Skills breakdown; check all that apply: ☐ Electrical engineering   ☐ Manufacturing engineering ☐ Software engineering   ☐ Other engineers, explain: ☐ Chemical engineering ☐ Mechanical engineering
Describe your company's OEM design experience:
Describe your company's experience with Underwriter's Laboratory (UL), Canada Standards Association (CSA), International Electrotechnical Commission (IEC), CE Mark, other than approvals:

C. Payments/invoicing terms

List payment/invoicing terms:

_____

List warranty/return policies:

_____

Provide contact name, email, and phone for accounts payable:

Name: _____

Phone: _____

E-mail: _____

Financial references or D&B information:

Name: _____

Phone: _____

E-mail: _____

Health and safety programs

Do you have a health and safety program? ☐ Yes ☐ No

Do you review your health and safety program on an annual basis to make sure that all local, state, and federal laws/requirements are being met? ☐ Yes ☐ No

Does your program follow all safety regulations, including training? ☐ Yes ☐ No

Do you document all accidents, incidents, and near misses? ☐ Yes ☐ No

Do you have an active safety committee? ☐ Yes ☐ No

Environmental programs

Do you have an environmental program in place, such as ISO 14001 environmental management or equivalent? ☐ Yes ☐ No

Do you review your environmental programs/aspects on an annual basis to make sure that all local, state, and federal laws/requirements are being met? ☐ Yes ☐ No

Please detail the elements of your environmental program below:

_____

_____

_____

D. System control questions *(Mark each question yes, no, or NA)*

1.0 Management system standard and metrics of the organization. (Add your own questions based on your industry and regulatory or conformity standards.)	Yes	No	NA
1.1	☐	☐	☐
1.2	☐	☐	☐
1.3	☐	☐	☐
1.4	☐	☐	☐
1.5	☐	☐	☐
1.6	☐	☐	☐
1.7	☐	☐	☐
1.8	☐	☐	☐
1.9	☐	☐	☐

Supply Chain Glossary

acceptance sampling—The practice of picking a sample at random from a lot, batch, or group. On the basis of information that is yielded by the sample, a decision should be made regarding the disposition of the lot. The decision generally is either to accept or reject the lot. This process is called lot acceptance sampling or just acceptance sampling. (Source: *Government Engineering Statistics Handbook,* section 6.2.1, What is acceptance sampling?)

bundling—A purchasing strategy that involves combining several "buys" on a single request for quotation (RFQ) and sending it to potential bidders rather than sending separate RFQs for each buy. The successful bidder is then awarded all the work.

business continuity plan—A document specifying tasks or activities needed to ensure that critical business functions in an organization will be available to customers, suppliers, regulators, and other entities that must have access to those functions.

commodity—A class of goods for which there is demand but which is supplied without qualitative differentiation across a market.

contract—An agreement entered into voluntarily by two or more parties with the intention of creating a legal obligation. It may have elements in writing, although contracts can be made orally.

corrective action—The implementation of solutions resulting in the reduction or elimination of an identified problem.

C_{pK} index—Equals the lesser or the upper specification limit (USL) minus the mean divided by three sigma (or the mean) minus the lower specification limit (LSL) divided by three sigma. The greater the C_{pK} value, the less variation in the process.

critical product or service—A product or service of major importance to the strategic or organizational objectives of an organization or to the functionality of a product or service.

critical requirements—Specifications that are vital or necessary to a product or service.

dashboard—Visuals used in manufacturing to identify good or poor performance of a process.

distributor—A middleman between a manufacturer and retailer or customer.

dock-to-stock—A program by which specific quality and packaging requirements are met before a product is released. Prequalified product is shipped directly into a customer's inventory. Dock-to-stock eliminates the costly handling of components, specifically in receiving and inspection, and enables product to move directly into production. (Source: www.apics.org/dictionary/dictionary-information?ID=1224 - 8k, 4/8/2013)

enterprise resource planning (ERP)—Systems that integrate and automate internal and external management of information across an entire organization, including finance and accounting, manufacturing, sales and service, and customer relationship management, using an integrated software application.

evergreen contract—An agreement between two parties that is automatically renewed after each maturity period until canceled by either party.

first-article inspection—1) The practice of inspecting the first item, part, unit, group, or batch produced from a production run. The results of the first-article inspection may be used to approve product for shipment, allow the process to continue, or call for the process to be adjusted and re-inspected. 2) A complete, independent, and documented physical and functional inspection process to verify that prescribed production methods have produced an acceptable item as specified by engineering drawings, planning, purchase order, engineering specifications, and/or other applicable design documents. (Source: AS 9102 Rev A)

flow-down requirement—A supplier requirement that must be passed down or delegated to sub-tier suppliers. Material or service specifications are often flowed down or passed down to the supplier's suppliers.

MilSpec—Specifications developed and used by the U.S. Department of Defense prior to commercialization in 1990. Most of these have been superseded.

one-off documents—Unique requirements for one contract not expected to be used again; for example, documents used or to be used only one time, such as instructions, specifications, and drawings for a particular job, project, or shop order.

original equipment manufacturer (OEM)—The organization at the top of the manufacturing supply chain that provides final product to end users.

packager—Function or entity that encloses products for distribution, storage, sale, and use.

pick to light—Digital selection and classification applied in manufacturing processes, warehousing, and distribution processes to direct operators, often for order fulfillment.

primes—A term used in some industries to identify the organizations at the top of their supply chain. Common in the construction industry as the contractor in charge of all the other contractors and responsible to the owner for project delivery.

processor—A manufacturer that converts a product from one form to another.

purchase order (PO)—A commercial document issued by a buyer to a seller that indicates types, quantities, and agreed prices for products or services the seller will provide to the buyer.

request for information (RFI)—An inquiry to a potential supplier about that supplier's product or service for potential use in the organization. The inquiry can provide certain organization requirements or be of a more general exploratory nature. (Source: www.apics.org/dictionary/dictionary-information?ID=3456)

request for proposal (RFP)—1) A method of soliciting ideas from potential suppliers that may be incorporated into a final design of a product or service for a later quote. 2) A document used to solicit vendor responses when the functional requirements and features are known but no specific product is in mind. (Source: www.apics.org/dictionary/dictionary-information?ID=3457)

request for quotation (RFQ)—An invitation to suppliers to bid on specific products or services. (Source: www.apics.org/dictionary/dictionary-information?ID=3522)

reverse auctions—An Internet auction in which suppliers attempt to underbid their competitors. Company identities are known only by the buyer. (Source: www.apics.org/dictionary/dictionary-information?ID=3510)

reverse pricing model—A model that allows the customer/consumer to establish his/her requirements and offer those requirements for bid by the seller. The customer instead of the supplier may propose a price for a transaction. Thus, rather than the seller marketing a product to the buyer, the reverse occurs.

risk management—Coordinated activities to direct and control an organization with regard to risk (risk is defined as effect of uncertainty on objectives). (Source: ISO Guide 73:2009, definition 2.1)

safety stock—Also called buffer stock, safety stock is a level of extra stock that is maintained to mitigate risk of shortfall in raw materials or packaging. It is the stock held by a company in excess of its requirement for the lead time.

skip lot inspection—A method of inspection in which only a portion, perhaps one-half or one-fourth, of the lots offered for inspection are actually inspected.

specification—An explicit set of requirements to be satisfied by a material, product, or service.

spend—Cost to an organization for a given purchased product or service for a specified period of time.

spot buy—A type of contract used for a one-time purchase.

standards developing organization (SDO)—An organization with the scope of establishing national, regional, or international standards.

statistical process control (SPC)—The application of statistical techniques to control a process. The term statistical quality control is often used interchangeably with it.

sub-tier supplier or supplier's supplier—A supplier for the main supplier of a product of service.

supplier—A source of materials, service, or information input provided to a process. (Source: ASQ online glossary, page 59, http://rube.asq.org/pub/qualityprogress/past/0702/qp0702glossary.pdf)

sustainability—Sometimes described as the triple bottom line, it is a process by which organizations manage their financial, social, and environmental risks, obligations, and opportunities.

tear-down—A method of estimating the real cost of competing products by understanding their design. Tear-down can involve tracking and use of data on costs such as those for raw materials and labor by region.

tooling—The portion of process machinery that is specific to a component or subassembly.

traceability—The ability to trace the history, application, or location of what is under consideration. When considering product, traceability can relate to the origin of materials and parts, the processing history, and the distribution and location of the product after delivery. (Source: ISO 9000:2005, clause 3.5.4)

validation—Assurance that the processes, machines, and materials used will produce conforming goods and services. Often used in regulated industries, where safety to the consuming public is of great concern.

value added—1) The parts of a process that add worth from the perspective of the external customer. 2) The value added to or created in a product or commodity by the manufacturing or marketing process exclusive of the cost of materials, supplies, packaging or overhead. (Source: *Webster's Third New International Dictionary*, unabridged, http://unabridged.merriam-webster.com)

value stream mapping—A pencil-and-paper tool used in two stages. Stage one follows a product's production path from beginning to end and visually represents every process in the material and information flows. Stage two then features the drawing of a future state map of how value should flow. The most important step is the future state map.

vendor managed inventory (VMI)—A supply chain business model in which risk is shared by having the organization purchasing a product provide information to the supplier of that product and the supplier then take full responsibility for maintaining an agreed-on inventory of the material.

vertical integration—The unification of a supply chain through common ownership. Usually each member of the supply chain produces a different product or service, and the products combine to satisfy a common need.

volume—The quantity needed by a purchasing organization for a specified product or service, typically included on a request for quotation and a contract.

Bibliography

ANSI/ISO/ASQ Q9001-2008, *Quality management systems–Requirements.* ASQ Quality Press, 2008.

ANSI/ISO/ASQ Q9004-2009, *Quality management systems–Managing for the sustained success of an organization.* ASQ Quality Press, 2009.

Besterfield, D. H., Besterfield, M. C., & Besterfield, G. H. *Total Quality Management Revised, 3rd Edition.* Pearson Education, 2011.

Blackstone Jr, J. H., & Jonah, J. *APICS Dictionary, 13th Edition.* APICS (The Association for Operations Management), 2010.

Bossert, J. L. *Supplier Management Handbook, 6th Edition.* ASQ Quality Press, 2004.

Burt, D. N., Dobler, D. W., & Starling, S. L. *World Class Supply Management, The Key to Supply Chain Management.* McGraw-Hill, 2006.

Gryna, R. C. *Juran's Quality Planning & Analysis for Enterprise Quality, 5th Edition.* ASQ Quality Press, 2010.

Gryna, R., Chua, H. C., & Defeo, J. A. *Juran's Quality Planning & Analysis for Enterprise Quality, 5th Edition.* McGraw-Hill College, 2005.

Handfield, R. B., Monczka, R. M., & Giunipero, L. C. *Sourcing and Supply Chain Management, 5th Edition.* South-Western, Cengage Learning, 2009.

Hill, A. V. *The Encyclopedia of Operations Management.* Pearson Education, Inc., 2012.

(IAPWG), I. P. *UN Procurement Practitioner's Handbook.* Interagency Procurement Working Group (IAPWG), 2006.

Juran, J. M., & De Feo, J. A. *Juran's Quality Handbook, 6th Edition.* McGraw-Hill, 2010.

Khurshid, Z. A. Selecting right vendor in accordance with Technology Strategy. *2nd Middle East Quality Congress.* Dubai: TQM College, 2008.

Khurshid, Z. A. Value Propositions as Enablers in Strategic Sourcing. *3rd Middle East Quality Congress.* Dubai: TQM College, 2009.

Library, J. M. Uniform Commercial Code. *Research Guide.* 2011.

Louise Bildsten, J. R. Applying the Kraljic model to the construction sector: The case of a Prefab housing factory. *Procs 26th Annual ARCOM Conference* (pp. 1029-1037). Leeds, UK: Association of Researchers in Construction Management, 2010.

Novak, Paul. Principles and Standards of Ethical Supply Management Conduct With Guidelines. *ISM Principles of Sustainability and Social Responsibility with a Guide to Adoption and Implementation.* Institute for Supply Management, Inc., 2012.

Scott, C., Lundgren, H., & Thompson, P. *Guide to Supply Chain Management.* Springer Berlin Heidelberg, 2011.

Zubair, A. K. Cost of Quality of Judicial Process. *2nd Middle East Quality Congress.* Dubai: TQM College, 2008.

Zubair, A. K. Selecting right vendor in accordance with Technology Strategy. *2nd Middle East Quality Congress.* Dubai: TQM College, 2008.

Zubair, A. K. Value Propositions as Enablers in Strategic Sourcing. *3rd Middle East Quality Congress.* Dubai: TQM College, 2009.

Index

Page numbers in *italics* refer to figures or tables.

The Knowledge Center
www.asq.org/knowledge-center

Learn about quality. Apply it. Share it.

ASQ's online Knowledge Center is the place to:

- Stay on top of the latest in quality with Editor's Picks and Hot Topics.

- Search ASQ's collection of articles, books, tools, training, and more.

- Connect with ASQ staff for personalized help hunting down the knowledge you need, the networking opportunities that will keep your career and organization moving forward, and the publishing opportunities that are the best fit for you.

Use the Knowledge Center Search to quickly sort through hundreds of books, articles, and other software-related publications.

www.asq.org/knowledge-center

TRAINING CERTIFICATION CONFERENCES MEMBERSHIP **PUBLICATIONS**

The Global Voice of Quality™

Ask a Librarian

Did you know?

- The ASQ Quality Information Center contains a wealth of knowledge and information available to ASQ members and non-members

- A librarian is available to answer research requests using ASQ's ever-expanding library of relevant, credible quality resources, including journals, conference proceedings, case studies and Quality Press publications

- ASQ members receive free internal information searches and reduced rates for article purchases

- You can also contact the Quality Information Center to request permission to reuse or reprint ASQ copyrighted material, including journal articles and book excerpts

- For more information or to submit a question, visit **http://asq.org/knowledge-center/ask-a-librarian-index**

Visit www.asq.org/qic for more information.

ASQ

The Global Voice of Qualit

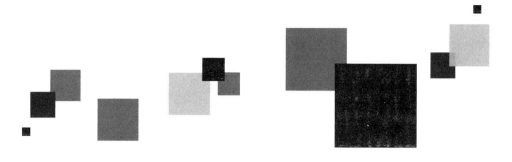

Belong to the Quality Community!

Established in 1946, ASQ is a global community of quality experts in all fields and industries. ASQ is dedicated to the promotion and advancement of quality tools, principles, and practices in the workplace and in the community.

The Society also serves as an advocate for quality. Its members have informed and advised the U.S. Congress, government agencies, state legislatures, and other groups and individuals worldwide on quality-related topics.

Vision

By making quality a global priority, an organizational imperative, and a personal ethic, ASQ becomes the community of choice for everyone who seeks quality technology, concepts, or tools to improve themselves and their world.

ASQ is...

- More than 90,000 individuals and 700 companies in more than 100 countries

- The world's largest organization dedicated to promoting quality

- A community of professionals striving to bring quality to their work and their lives

- The administrator of the Malcolm Baldrige National Quality Award

- A supporter of quality in all sectors including manufacturing, service, healthcare, government, and education

- YOU

Visit www.asq.org for more information.

TRAINING CERTIFICATION CONFERENCES MEMBERSHIP **PUBLICATIONS**

ASQ Membership

Research shows that people who join associations experience increased job satisfaction, earn more, and are generally happier*. ASQ membership can help you achieve this while providing the tools you need to be successful in your industry and to distinguish yourself from your competition. So why wouldn't you want to be a part of ASQ?

Networking

Have the opportunity to meet, communicate, and collaborate with your peers within the quality community through conferences and local ASQ section meetings, ASQ forums or divisions, ASQ Communities of Quality discussion boards, and more.

Professional Development

Access a wide variety of professional development tools such as books, training, and certifications at a discounted price. Also, ASQ certifications and the ASQ Career Center help enhance your quality knowledge and take your career to the next level.

Solutions

Find answers to all your quality problems, big and small, with ASQ's Knowledge Center, mentoring program, various e-newsletters, *Quality Progress* magazine, and industry-specific products.

Access to Information

Learn classic and current quality principles and theories in ASQ's Quality Information Center (QIC), *ASQ Weekly* e-newsletter, and product offerings.

Advocacy Programs

ASQ helps create a better community, government, and world through initiatives that include social responsibility, Washington advocacy, and Community Good Works.

Visit www.asq.org/membership for more information on ASQ membership.

*2008, The William E. Smith Institute for Association Research

The Global Voice of Quali